Edited by

Brendan Leahy and Declan Marmion

GW00633973

Faith Questions

the columba press

First published in 2013 by

the columba press

55A Spruce Avenue, Stillorgan Industrial Park,
Blackrock, Co. Dublin

Cover by Patrick O'Donoghue
Origination by The Columba Press
Printed by MPG Printgroup Ltd.

ISBN 978 1 78218 040 1

Table of Contents

Note on Contributors

Dr Martin Henry is a priest of the diocese of Down and Connor in Northern Ireland, and has been a lecturer in Dogmatic Theology in St Patrick's College Maynooth since 1982. His research interests include: the modern God question, nineteenth-century Protestant theology, in particular, the work of Franz Overbeck.

Prof. Brendan Leahy is former Professor of Systematic Theology at St Patrick's College, Maynooth and has been recently appointed Bishop of Limerick.

Dr Declan Marmion, SM, is Lecturer in Systematic Theology at St Patrick's College, Maynooth. His research interests include the theology of Karl Rahner and trinitarian theology.

Dr Mary McCaughey lectures in Systematic Theology at St Patrick's College, Maynooth, All Hallows, Dublin and is Co-ordinator of Religion with Hibernia College. Her research interests are Ecclesiology, Mariology and the Reception of Revelation.

Dr Noel O'Sullivan is a priest of the diocese of Cork and Ross. His research interests include the theology of Henri de Lubac and the theology of the priesthood.

Dr Oliver Treanor is a priest of the diocese of Down and Connor and teaches Systematic Theology at the Pontifical University, Maynooth. His research interests include ecclesiology and eucharistic theology.

Introduction:
Exploring Faith Questions

When we look up to the sky at night we are captivated by the vast array of stars. The more we gaze, the more our wonder grows. Some people study what they are seeing. They explore the constellations and galaxies. They read up on the Big Bang theory. They want to know about the expanding universe. The more they know, the more their excitement grows, the deeper their appreciation for what they are seeing.

Faith is something like that. For those who have the gift, it is a light that shines in their lives. The more they explore and investigate their faith, the more the excitement and profound enchantment grows. The Letter to the Hebrews tells us that 'faith is the assurance of things hoped for, the conviction of things not seen' (Heb 11:1).

It has been said that faith and reason are two wings on which we rise to contemplate the Truth. Using our reason we seek to clarify points about what and why it is we believe. Issues arise that make us ask questions we hadn't thought of before. Our explorations become a spur to deepen our faith both in terms of the knowledge of the contents but also in terms of our response to the God who has loved us first. Faith always seeks understanding.

There are many today who claim they do not have the gift of faith. Often they ask their companions who do believe to explain their faith to them. St Peter writes that we must always be ready to give reasons for the hope we have in us.

In this short book, a number of contributors from the Systematic Department of St Patrick's College offer reflections on various aspects of Christian faith. Each chapter is short. It allows for either personal study or group reflection.

In pursuing questions of faith a thirst of our mind is quenched and the desire to live out our faith is strengthened.

Faith sends us out in love towards others. As Pope Francis has shown so clearly, faith makes us become protectors of one another, of the poor and of creation.

1

How do we come to know God?

Noel O'Sullivan

If God is total mystery is there any point in trying to get to know him? Is it possible for finite human beings to penetrate the mystery of God? And yet God came among us in the person of Jesus Christ; how do we connect with him?

We are sometimes tempted to think that it must have been easy for those who met Jesus face-to-face in first century Palestine. And, yet, we read in the Gospels that only a minority recognised him for who he was; many walked away from him, finding his claims too hard to take. Others sought to kill him because he threatened the religious equilibrium of the day; the crowd succeeded in having him crucified. Recognizing Jesus for who he was is not all that obvious, even among his friends and acquaintances. I don't think we are at any greater disadvantage than they were. The challenge we face is similar to theirs: how do we recognise God? How do we come to know him? Where do we look; how do we go about it?

One approach to this question is to think about how we come to know another person. Two things are essential in that process: the other person must be willing to be known and we need to spend time with them, allowing ourselves to be known in turn. It is very much a two-way process.

Applying that human experience to our relationship with God allows us to see certain parallels and, of course, radical differences. First of all, does God let himself be known? Yes, he does in two different ways. One way is through creation, that is, both nature and other people. The other way is through what we technically call 'revelation'.

Revelation is the lifting of the veil that enables us to get glimpses of God but the veil is never removed completely so that our knowledge of God is always partial. This revelation is not a personal revelation to each person individually but, rather, to humanity as a whole through human history. The great events of God's people in the Old Testament were experiences of revelation. This is true of creation itself, for example. Through creation God shares his beauty and love with us. The high point of God's self-disclosure in Jewish history was the liberation from slavery in Egypt, which Jews to this day regard as God coming to their rescue. This event is called the 'Exodus' and is believed to have taken place about 1250 BC. But for Christians God's definitive self-revelation came in the person of Jesus Christ.

The coming of Christ into the world is the high point of God's self-disclosure. The French Jesuit, Cardinal Henri de Lubac (1896–1991) described the Incarnation as God bursting forth into human history, and changing it forever. The Incarnation is the technical term we use for God becoming man. The Father and the Holy Spirit did not become man; it was the Son, the second person of the Trinity, who became human, the man we call Jesus Christ. So the primary way in which we get to know God is through Jesus Christ. We can learn much about Jesus by reading the scriptures, especially the four Gospels but we also learn about Jesus from the teaching of the Church. This teaching ensures that we are getting to know the real Jesus and not some human image that we create ourselves. But it is not just a matter of learning about Jesus; we can come to know him personally as our friend: 'I have called you friends, because I have made known to you everything that I have heard from my Father' (Jn 15:15). Essential to coming to know Jesus as friend is personal prayer. Time spent in his presence, especially before the Blessed Sacrament in the tabernacle or exposed on the altar, is what deepens this relationship. We do not even need to use words; just be there, like two lovers sitting in the reassuring presence of each other. The rays of love that emanate from the tabernacle deepen our faith, heal our wounds of sin and hurt, and enable us to become like Him. 'The life of prayer is the habit of being in the presence of the thrice-holy God and in communion with him' (*Catechism of the Catholic Church* 2565).

There are two important caveats to keep in mind. The first is the danger of individualism: the tendency to see our relationship with God as exclusive; a cosy, private affair between 'Jesus and me'. The whole thrust of Christianity is that it is a community. It is in our relationships with other people that our relationship with God evolves. The second potential pitfall is the exclusion of mystery. God comes close to us in Jesus (God with us) but he is still the unknowable other. St Augustine (354–430) cautions against the presumption of thinking that we know God: when we claim to have understood God it is not God whom we have understood. Augustine writes: 'If you understand, it is not God. If you are able to understand, you understand something other than God' (*Sermo* 117, 5).

2

In what sense is God 'Father'?

Brendan Leahy

The opening line of the Creed says that 'we believe in God the Father almighty, creator of heaven and earth'. In what sense is God 'Father'? In what sense is he 'almighty'? When Jesus recommended we put all our trust in God the Father was he presenting a paternalistic God that doesn't take human responsibility seriously? Is the notion of 'Father' not patriarchal language? Should we not also call God 'Mother'?

A reading of the Gospels, especially John's, reveals how Jesus' life revolved around his relationship with the one he called, in his Aramaic language, 'Abba'. This term speaks of trust, utter confidence in God's care and closeness, abandonment to God as to a father or mother. The use and frequency of this familiar calling on God distinguishes Jesus from his contemporaries.

Jesus sensed he had a unique relationship with God. He was the son who had the unique role of bringing others to share in the kingdom of God. And so, in drawing close to sinners, outsiders and people in all kinds of situations of darkness, Jesus proclaimed 'good news' that God is a Father who is always ready to forgive, reinstate sinners as his children and even hold a celebration for them when they turn around, believe and trust in him. We see this for instance in what is often called the parable of the Prodigal Son (Lk 15:11–32).

But that doesn't mean God is paternalistic. It's enough to consider the parable of the Talents. In that parable we see how God wants us to be fully alive, mature, responsible human beings, developing our talents, bringing ahead this world that has been created as a gift for us and we for it! God is also just.

When Christians call God 'Father' they recognise their God is not anonymous or a faceless divinity, but rather an infinite, divine 'I' who addresses us as 'you' and whom we can speak to as 'you'. Jesus wanted to bring us into a deeply *personal* relationship with God the Father in a new and radical sense. His use of 'Abba' was a characteristic feature of his prayer and he wanted to make of our whole life a constant sharing in his prayer to the Father. And that would lead to radical social and interpersonal consequences as we see in the 'Our Father' prayer (Mt 6:9; Lk 11:2), the Sermon on the Mount (Mt 5–7) and the commandment to love our neighbour (Mk 12:30–31).

To really understand God as Father we have to let Jesus introduce us into what he meant. Otherwise, we are simply projecting our notions of fatherhood (which always have limitations) onto God. Already in the Old Testament it is clearly stated that God as such is not male. He is neither male nor female.

While we come to know God the Father through Jesus, it is also true that our human experience helps us to understand what Jesus reveals about him. Pope John Paul II pointed out that when it comes to understanding the fatherhood of God as revealed by Jesus Christ we have to keep in mind our experience of both fatherhood *and* motherhood. It is true, then, that Jesus left us the language of 'Father' but it is to be understood, experienced and believed in and through him. And he reveals both paternal and maternal dimensions of God. It is worth recalling how on earth, Mary is the one who best mirrored God the Father for Jesus.

On the question of the 'almighty' God, it is important to remember that God's omnipotence is no abstract power. In God, omnipotence, creativity and mercy, love and justice all coincide. This means that in all situations God is working always on all these levels as it were. At any one moment, we might not sense God is really almighty. For instance we might feel he isn't answering our prayers. But in each moment all of God's creative, freeing, merciful and justice-building power is at work. We see this most clearly in Jesus' death and resurrection: 'God raised him up, having freed him from death' (Acts 2:24). It might certainly have seemed to Jesus on the Cross that God wasn't answering his prayers. It might have seemed God was powerless. And yet God was working powerfully through Jesus precisely as he lay dying on the Cross. Then, in the Resurrection, God raised Jesus from the dead.

Our belief in 'God the Father almighty' also implies recognizing the universality of God's overarching plan for humanity and the cosmos. It calls us to be aware that as sons and daughters of God entrusted with stewardship of creation, we have ecological responsibility towards creation.

To believe in God the Father is to believe in One Father of many children, all brothers and sisters to one another. It is to believe that we can cast all our worries onto the Father because, as St Paul writes: 'For I am convinced that neither death, nor life … nor depth, nor anything else in all creation, will be able to separate us from the love of God in Christ Jesus our Lord' (Rom 8:38–39).

3

How rational is belief in 'creation'?

Martin Henry

Christianity is unthinkable without a doctrine of creation; hence an inevitable question that must be faced is: How rational is belief in 'creation'?

The Christian doctrine of creation states that God created the world from nothing, or *ex nihilo,* to use the traditional Latin expression. As a doctrine it was widely accepted in the church from the end of the second century and became official church teaching at the Fourth Lateran Council (1215), being restated at the First Vatican Council (1870).

It is the first article of the (Apostles') Creed. As such, it is primarily a matter of faith or belief rather than of knowledge. But that is not by any means to say it is irrational. In other words, while it may not be possible to arrive at the doctrine of 'creation out of nothing' by reason alone, that is not the same thing as to say that the doctrine is irrational.

The best-known Catholic medieval thinker, St Thomas Aquinas, certainly relied on revelation to anchor the Christian doctrine of creation. He apparently didn't consider that reason alone could prove the truth of such a belief. In line with the views of his main philosophical mentor from antiquity, Aristotle, he regarded belief in the eternity of the world as being also compatible with reason. But Aquinas did not regard belief in creation as being incompatible with reason. In fact his famous 'five ways' (of demonstrating God's existence) were devoted to fulfilling precisely the task of showing the reasonableness and indeed rationality of belief in God as the transcendent creator and sustaining source of the world.

In the earliest times of the church, belief in creation was indeed regarded as a matter of faith. Thus we read in the New Testament, in the Letter to the Hebrews (11:3): 'By faith we understand that the world was created by the word of God, so that what is seen was made out of things which do not appear.' However, even the biblical witness does not neglect the question of the reasonable nature of belief in God the Creator. Both the Old Testament (as the wisdom literature, specifically, demonstrates) and the New Testament (St Paul's writings, in particular) assume that God can be known from the traces he has left of his creative activity in the world. This was a view most recently officially endorsed at the First Vatican Council, to which reference has already been made, where it was solemnly decreed

> that God, the beginning and end of all things, can be known with certainty from the things that were created through the natural light of human reason, for 'ever since the creation of the world His invisible nature has been clearly perceived in the things that have been made' (Rom 1:20) (J. Neuner, SJ & J. Dupuis, SJ [eds.], *The Christian Faith*, p. 43).

And in post-biblical times, it wasn't long before early Christian thinkers began developing a so-called 'natural theology' in order to argue in favour of the plausibility of belief in the doctrine of creation *ex nihilo*. For while they of course saw Scripture as the Book of God, providing knowledge of God, they also regarded the cosmos (the 'Book of Nature', as it came to be called) as providing reliable knowledge of the Creator.

In their generally affirmative assessment of the created order as good, the early Christian theologians found allies in the Hellenistic or Greek-speaking pagan intellectuals of late antiquity. The latter, like the Christians, rejected the idea that the world had been created by an evil demiurge (or creator), even though they didn't accept the Christian explanation of the world as created by God *ex nihilo*. But it may have been partly the sense of the ordered nature of the world (the Greek word *kosmos* means 'order'), pointing for the Christians to the ultimate source of order, who is God, that kindled Christian zeal for Platonic thought.

The notion of creation fits in fact quite easily with reasoned attempts to argue from the existence of a contingent or totally dependent world to the existence of a self-existent Being who is responsible for the world's existence. This is the heart of the so-called cosmological argument for the existence of God. And such traditional arguments can be supplemented by the more modern approach of appealing to the human experience of contingency as an argument for the plausibility of the doctrine of creation *ex nihilo*.

Developing the notion of humanity's sense of its absolute dependence on a sublime reality beyond it, Rudolf Otto (1869–1937) spoke of 'creature-consciousness' or the human awareness of God as the *mysterium tremendum et fascinans* ('fearful and fascinating mystery'), inspiring dread and fascination. 'It is', he writes, 'the emotion of a creature, abased and overwhelmed by its own nothingness in contrast to that which is supreme above all creatures' (*The Idea of the Holy*, p. 10).

When people nowadays say they don't believe in God, what they may actually mean is that they don't think the world has a creator or a transcendent, sustaining origin. Rather, they think that the world is just 'there'. If this view is correct, then the world is simply a 'given' with,

somewhat paradoxically, no 'giver'. And the world's existence would or could, then, raise no questions about its ultimate origin or goal.

4

Does evil have an explanation?

Martin Henry

One of the most persistent causes of atheism or at least of serious doubt about God's existence is the presence of evil in the world. How, in a world created by God, who is believed to be infinitely good, can the emergence of evil be explained?

The problem of evil, especially in the form of the suffering of the innocent, is not only as old as the Bible, but indeed the Bible itself is primarily driven by a need to face up to this problem. Another way of saying the same thing is to suggest that both Judaism and Christianity, like all religions perhaps, are responses to the burning theological problem of evil. And, finally, it could be argued that serious theology has at heart always tended to be a form of theodicy, that is to say, a reasoned defence of the justice of God in the face of the perennial problem of evil and suffering.

The actual term 'theodicy' itself is of fairly recent coinage. It first appeared in 1710 in a work published by the German philosopher, G.W. Leibniz, and ever since has been widely used in theology. But before Leibniz, theologians of course attempted to deal in different ways with the problem of evil. The Bible itself, as claimed above, can be read as one long essay in theodicy, since its main thrust is to present a statement of faith in the possibility of the redemption of the world by God, despite the human difficulty of understanding how this can be achieved.

What, then, does theology have to say about the problem of evil? The first thing to be said is that the tension between faith and reason has always been particularly acute in the area described in 2 Thessalonians 2:7 as 'the mystery of iniquity.' For evil seems to offer an insoluble problem to a religion like Christianity that proclaims its belief in an omnipotent, good and benevolent God who, without any compulsion, freely created a world in which evil and suffering are ever-present.

The problem can be quickly stated: if God is both all good and all-powerful, he should be able to deal with evil. If evil persists, it can apparently only be because God is either not all good, and hence is not in fact concerned with eliminating evil, or he is not all-powerful, and hence, while he may in his goodness wish to eliminate evil, he lacks the wherewithal to do so. Thus, he cannot be God as Christian faith conceives God to be. Suffering has thus been described as the rock on which atheism is founded.

In the opening chapter of his book *Religion*, the late Polish philosopher, Leszek Kołakowski, scrutinizes the problem of evil and concludes that all theodicies are in fact doomed to failure: they do not prove that the co-existence of a good and omnipotent creator with a world containing untold horror and anguish is a rationally demonstrable state of affairs involving no self-contradictory elements. Yet he doesn't deduce from this conclusion that theodicy as such is pointless. Rather, the fact that people bother constructing theodicies at all is for him a matter of profound significance. For it testifies, in his judgement, to the human instinct to find a just order within the cosmos, and hence to a hope that, despite all appearances to the contrary, justice and goodness will ultimately triumph and evil be defeated.

In short, the existence of theodicies springs from a belief that people's lives are not the absurd playthings of a blind, inexorable, meaningless fate, as they are, for example, in the philosophy of Schopenhauer.

The existence of theodicy or the unwillingness to abandon the attempt to understand how God's goodness can be seen to operate in the chaos of history, this – in Kołakowski's view – amounts to an affirmation of the religious conviction that God is good and omnipotent and that what he has created has an order deep within or behind it. Believers choose to endorse this order, while trying, at the same time, to resist evil and not to give intellectual assent to the notion of meaninglessness and absurdity.

Hence, the human need for theodicy bears witness to the conviction (or faith) that meaning in life and history, what ultimately constitutes meaning for humanity, is connected with the difference between good and evil. Theodicy, in other words, flows from faith, not the other way about. Now, since God *is* the good, and since evil is only definable derivatively from the good (and is not good's equal, as in 'dualism'), theodicy, in revealing a human instinct to look for meaning where good and evil come into conflict, also reveals that, for Christianity, the ultimate judge of what constitutes meaning is God, without whom the distinction between good and evil disappears.

In short, the 'problem of evil' is itself a religious expression, and to use it is, at least implicitly, to be locked into a religious world view. To say, with the French nineteenth-century writer Stendhal, that 'God's only excuse is that he does not exist', would be to abandon belief in the ultimate significance of terms like good and evil. The Christian hope, of course, is that good can stand alone, whereas evil cannot.

But for those who do not believe in a good God, evil ceases – like 'good,' too, it should be added – to have any substantial significance. The difference between good and evil would then be simply swallowed up in the value-free flow of history.

5

Are science and religion compatible?

Noel O'Sullivan

Ever since the Copernican revolution began in the 16th century there has been suspicion and, at times, outright opposition between religion and science. Even in recent times some high profile commentators have claimed that religion and science are incompatible; that science is the only reliable conduit to truth. The publication of Richard Dawkin's The God Delusion *(2006) and the discovery of the* Higgs Bosun *(2012) brought this question to the forefront of public debate.*

Six Day Creation Story and the Big Bang Theory

Few questions focus the mind on the relationship between religion and science as that of the origin of the universe. For centuries the presumption was that the six day creation story in the Book of Genesis described how the world came about. Then science suggested the hypothesis that the world developed in an evolutionary way, leading to the human being as the highest point of evolution. Furthermore, it claimed that this development took place through natural selection, with only the fittest surviving. A critical date was the publication by Charles Darwin of his book on natural selection, *On the Origin of Species*, in 1859. Darwin's work was regarded as a challenge to the Book of Genesis. Furthermore, the question of the origin of the universe itself and the answer offered by science set religion and science on a collision course. How could the Big Bang Theory (first proposed by a Belgian priest-scientist, Fr Lemaître, in 1927) be compatible with the religious view that God created the world?

Reconciliation between religion and science was eventually made possible when scripture came to be understood in its original meaning. The Bible is not a work of science or history in the modern sense. It is a religious document whose authors – inspired by God – give a religious interpretation of life. Their concern is to communicate who God and, as a consequence, how we can understand the origin and meaning of human life. The sacred authors used the knowledge and language that were available to them as far back as 3,000 years ago. In relation to the origin of the universe they do not attempt to tell us how the world was created, because they didn't know. Instead, they composed religious poetry and other literary constructs to enable them to explain the meaning of human existence. The six day creation story is a religious poem which expresses very profound truths about the nature and purpose of creation. The poem explains that the universe had its origin in God and that all of creation is good, with the human being as the highest point of creation. And God created all manner of species effortlessly. This contrasted with similar stories or myths about origins in the surrounding culture whereby the universe was understood as being the result of conflict between the gods, with the resultant creation being of its nature evil.

Higgs Boson

Some loose media commentaries referred to the discovery of the Higgs Boson as the 'God particle', implying that God is no longer needed to explain the origin of the universe. But these commentators are misusing the title of a book written 20 years ago entitled, *The God Particle*. The author, Leon Lederman, intended the title merely as a metaphor, a way to describe the importance of this particular particle which, if discovered, would validate the Standard Model; a particle which, in its elegance, might reflect the elegance of God; and a particle whose existence, like that of God, its believers have had to take only on faith.

Science and religion have different functions which are complementary. They are both seeking the *one* truth. But they ask different sets of questions. Science asks questions that have simple and often quantifiable answers: how many? how big? what happens first? what happens next? There is another set of questions which we ponder all our lives, even when we already have answers for them; questions about meaning and beauty and love. Putting it simply, science tries to answer the question, how? Religion answers the question, why? We look to science to tell us *how* the world came to be; we turn to religion to tell us *why* there is a world at all and what meaning there is to human existence.

Pope Benedict XVI highlighted the complementary nature of the relationship between science and religion when he wrote: 'The Church has never been afraid of demonstrating that there cannot be any conflict between faith and genuine science, because both, albeit via different routes, tend towards the truth' (*Porta Fidei* 12). What the Pope emeritus said here is in the best tradition of the Church. In the thirteenth century, St Thomas Aquinas wrote: 'All truth, irrespective of who expresses it, comes from the Holy Spirit as the source of natural light and as exercising on the spirit of man a desire to grasp and speak what is true' (*Summa Theologiae*, I, II, q. 109, art. 1).

Science and religion are friends, good friends and they need each other.

6

What is Christian Faith?

Noel O'Sullivan

The term 'faith' can be used in a variety of contexts and, depending on the particular situation, it can vary considerably in its meaning. I can have faith in my rugby coach ... or in my doctor ... or in a particular remedy for the common cold. But the Christian faith? Its meaning is not immediately obvious. I will begin by looking at the human quest for religious faith and then move on in an attempt to understand it.

One question that I grapple with myself is why some people have faith and others do not. I am thinking of friends and parishioners who seem genuinely to want faith but, somehow, it eludes them. I was struck by the comments of the priest who celebrated the funeral Mass of popular fiction writer, Maeve Binchy. She is reported as having said to her parish priest: 'I know that if you are around when I die then you will dispatch me with dignity and without hypocrisy in a faith which I envy and would love to share.' The homilist at the funeral, Fr Stuart said: 'Maeve came from the tradition of the Magi. She was a searcher, a seeker of the divine, but it eluded her' (*The Irish Times*, 4 August 2012). That is an authentic place to be: genuinely searching but, disappointingly, not finding. It is also a very hard place to be. In his apostolic letter, introducing the year of faith,

Pope Benedict XVI commented on this search and called it a preamble to faith. This is what he said:

> Very many people, while not claiming to have the gift of faith, are nevertheless sincerely searching for the ultimate meaning and definitive truth of their lives and of the world. This search is an authentic 'preamble' to the faith, because it guides people onto the path that leads to the mystery of God (*Porta Fidei* 10).

This begs the question: what is faith?

Christian Faith

Faith is a response to Revelation. God has spoken; he has unveiled himself as Father, Son, and Holy Spirit and has invited human beings to share in that community of love. Though faith involves intellectual assent to certain truths, it is much more than that. It is the adherence of the whole person to God in the community of the Church.

The letter to the Hebrews defines faith as, 'the assurance of things hoped for, the conviction of things not seen' (Heb 11:1). This implies that the reality believed in is somehow beyond our grasp: we cannot see it; there is the implication that it has to do with something in the future.

Pope Benedict XVI defined faith as 'the act by which we choose to entrust ourselves fully to God, in complete freedom' (*Porta Fidei* 10). It is adherence to God; Father, Son, and Holy Spirit. The Pope emeritus said that the door of faith is always open to us,

> ushering us into the life of communion with God and offering entry into his Church. It is possible to cross that threshold when the word of God is proclaimed and the heart allows itself to be shaped by transforming grace (*Porta Fidei* 1).

Faith, then, is an entrusting of ourselves fully to God in total freedom. The life of faith is a life of communion with God, in his Church. It is an adherence of the heart as well as of the mind. Grace is essential to the act of faith. Faith is weakened by sin, especially the sin of pride.

I began with the question: why is it that some people are able to believe and others are not? I'm afraid there is no easy answer. We believe that God is only too willing to give faith to anyone who wants it. Sometimes people have faith and don't recognise it. Some people look for too much certainty. Faith is on occasion clear: yes, God is really there. But, more often than not, God seems distant and hidden. These are the times when we shouldn't panic and think: 'Oh, I've lost my faith!' No, this is more likely the time when our faith is really growing, like the seed sown secretly in the earth.

The apparent absence of God is often the moment when we are closest to God. The Christian mystics were keenly aware of that, especially St John of the Cross (1542–91). He expressed this insight in his poetry. These lines are taken from the beginning of the *Canticle*:

> Where have you hidden Beloved, and left me groaning?
> You fled like a stag having wounded me;
> I went out in search of you, and you were gone.

A life of faith is a life of relationship with God; Father, Son, and Holy Spirit. It is not primarily an intellectual assent to certain truths or beliefs; these come later. The starting point for faith is a relationship of love with the divine, with the One who has loved us first.

7

Are faith and the spirit of critical enquiry incompatible?

Declan Marmion

What does it mean to say that faith must be rational? Are faith and the scientific mentality incompatible? And how can theology deepen our understanding and appreciation of the Christian faith tradition?

Many opponents of religion, for example the scientist Richard Dawkins, maintain that religious faith and the spirit of critical enquiry are incompatible. Radical secularists like Dawkins actually show a complete intolerance for any form of religious world view other than their scientific model. For them, religion is equated with fundamentalism, superstition, or some other form of outmoded thinking. Diatribe and polemic replace dialogue as the *modus operandi*.

However, religious believers cannot be so easily categorised or dismissed. True, many Irish Catholics have received only a rudimentary catechesis or religious instruction in school which has left them ill-equipped to judge whether scientific advances are compatible with traditional Christian beliefs. This has led to scepticism and confusion in how to interpret the Bible and sometimes, unfortunately, to the view that Christian convictions, for example, about the origin and destiny of the universe are outdated. In fact, it could be said that the average Christian in Ireland today is likely to be better educated in almost any area other than their faith. On a more positive note, however, the growth in adult faith formation courses and evening courses in theology and Christian spirituality testifies to the desire for a deeper knowledge of faith and to the hunger for God. In such courses participants are introduced to the discipline of theology classically described by the eleventh-century theologian St Anselm as 'faith seeking understanding'.

Theology, then, assumes faith on which it reflects. As St Augustine said in the fourth century, *credo ut intelligam*, 'I believe in order that I may understand.' This 'committed' approach distinguishes theology from religious studies, where a more detached, quasi-neutral, approach is taken towards a variety of religions. At the same time, a committed perspective does not mean that reason plays only a minor role in the theological enterprise. On the contrary, as Pope John Paul II put it in the opening of his 1998 encyclical on faith and reason (*Fides et Ratio*), 'faith and reason are like two wings on which the human spirit rises to the contemplation of truth.'

Pope Benedict XVI took up and developed this theme of the pursuit of truth as the goal of theology. And for him *God* is the fullness of truth, goodness and beauty. Following Augustine, Pope Benedict showed how only God can satisfy the deepest desires of the human person. In this view of theology reason is valued but not overvalued.[1] With Benedict

---

[1] Benedict is more than aware of the gains of Enlightenment modernity including scientific progress, developments in democracy, and the rights of the individual. But, he is also aware of the limitations of the scientific paradigm and the role science has played in the destruction and suffering of war.

we could say that reason needs to be 'chastened'. Most of the great theologians in the Christian tradition – East and West – acknowledged this. From Thomas Aquinas to Karl Rahner we see a degree of humility and modesty when it comes to discussing the things of God.

Theology is rational discourse (Gk *logos*) about God (Gk *theos*) and humankind's relationship to God. And in this enterprise *both* faith and reason have a role to play. There is always the danger of a kind of anti-intellectualism when it comes to matters of faith and belief. But that only leaves us with a childish faith which is easily discarded when there is nothing deeper with which to replace it. It leads to distorted images of God and to simplistic caricatures of Scripture and the Christian tradition.

Studying theology, reflecting on our faith, enables us to critically appreciate our Christian heritage and provides us with resources to enrich our present. The Christian tradition is a bit like an attic in which all kinds of things have been stored. When we rummage around in it, we discover not only things we realise we should have discarded years ago, but also things we had long forgotten and which are still valuable. Theology is a journey of discovery where we explore the rich variety of our Christian tradition. And as thinking believers we approach this tradition in a spirit of critical appreciation or with what some theologians describe as a hermeneutics of generosity *and* a hermeneutics of suspicion. Not everything that was once part of the Christian tradition can be accepted today (e.g. slavery), yet the central Christian vision, namely, that God created the world out of love so that humanity might share in the life of God, endures. Believers, moreover, are called 'to give an account of the hope that is in us,' as the first letter of Peter (1 Pet 3:15) states. We might not be able to 'prove' the mysteries of our faith but we should be able to discuss them in a rational and coherent manner.

Theology, then, can lead us to a deeper and more adult understanding of our faith even if it can be disconcerting to have our cherished religious ideas from childhood 'deconstructed'. But ultimately such deconstruction is in the service of reconstruction. The love of learning and the desire for God are of a piece. Many of the outstanding theologians and doctors of the Church were also canonised saints, including Augustine, Thomas Aquinas, Bonaventure, and Catherine of Siena. Thus, far from undermining our religious convictions, respectful yet critical theological reflection will help us to discover our theological voice and better understand what it means to be a Christian today.

8

What is the link between faith and experience?

Declan Marmion

What is the connection between faith and experience? What kinds of experience are we referring to here? And are there dangers associated with an overly experiential approach to Christian faith?

Faith is linked to experience in a number of ways. In discussing and reflecting on their faith Christians will, inevitably and rightly, draw from their experience of what being a Christian means to them. Sometimes one hears it said about a particular Church teaching or doctrine: 'that's not my experience' or 'that doesn't resonate with me'. If the articulation of faith in formal Church teaching does not speak to people's experience, then it risks being dismissed or ignored. There has to be a link between doctrine – formulations of faith – and experience, but the interaction goes both ways. Often, when people say 'in my experience …' they are usually implying that whatever they say next cannot be contradicted, since it is 'my experience'. There is a danger here of an unqualified subjectivism or solipsism in matters of belief, where the bottom line is what 'feels right' to a person. It expresses a kind of postmodern relativism where almost anything goes, where what's true for you is true for you and what's true for me is true for me. The search for objective truth is abandoned. This eclectic approach to faith on the part of many of us indicates to what extent we are imbued with a postmodern mentality. Positively, it reflects a healthy suspicion of authority: nothing is true simply because an authority says it's true; the truth has to persuade, to convince, to resonate in order to be received. Its weakness, however, is making the individual the final arbiter in religious and moral decisions and not sufficiently acknowledging the role of ecclesial authority and tradition.

So we need to approach the notion of experience with a degree of caution as it is a slippery and ambiguous concept. If an uncritical exaltation of subjective experience is to be avoided, so is an approach to faith that begins from on high, from abstract principles, and deductively tries to apply these to life situations. When we are trying to understand a particular aspect of our faith, for example, the divinity of Jesus, we need to 'get behind' the doctrine, as it were. How did this conviction come about? What were the main issues at stake? Why was it so important for early Christians that Jesus was more than a human being? And finally, can the truth of such a dogma be expressed in a different way today so that it can be better 'received'? When we study and reflect on our tradition of faith we employ an interactive, dialogical approach: we talk to the tradition and it talks to us.

In referring to the importance of people's experiences we are really saying that faith must connect with life. Faith is about head, heart and feet. In other words, there are three dimensions to faith. There is the intellectual dimension: faith can be expressed in statements of belief; the affective dimension: faith is about a personal relationship or encounter with God; and a behavioural dimension: faith is not just about knowing the truth but doing the truth too.

The second dimension of faith alluded to above – the affective – points to our experience of God, which lies at the heart of the Christian understanding of faith. In other words, faith is not *primarily* about belief in doctrines but about an encounter with God, which gives rise to a new way of seeing things and a new way of living. This dynamic is at the heart of the New Testament stories of faith, for example, Zacchaeus the tax collector (Lk 19:1–10) who, after encountering Jesus, vowed to share his wealth and compensate those he defrauded. In other words, a genuine experience of God leads to a reformed way of life more attuned to the values of the Gospel.

The problem is trying to discern whether a particular experience is from God or from another source. The Christian tradition has long struggled with what it calls the 'discernment of spirits' – how do I know that it is really *God* who is calling me to this course of action or to this way of life? While the issue is complicated, we can say that a genuine experience of God will be manifest in fruits of the Spirit including love, joy, peace, forbearance, kindness, goodness, faithfulness, gentleness and self-control (Gal 5:22–23). Moreover, the 'experiences' we are thinking of here are not limited to moments of harmony, inner peace, or union with God. They also include negative experiences, for example, experiences of suffering or failure. Such experiences can be a prelude to an experience of God. Often it is only later that someone will acknowledge that God's hand was at work during a time of suffering. In his spiritual autobiography, the *Confessions*, St Augustine, looking back, was able to trace how God was present over the whole course of his life, including his various searches and their dead ends, gradually drawing him to Himself. And it is this God who wants to share life, a God who gives and receives, and who can be experienced, that lies at the heart of our faith.

9

How has the theology of faith changed since Vatican II?

Declan Marmion

How has the Church's understanding of faith changed? Is there more to faith than an intellectual adherence to certain doctrines? How are we to understand the affective and behavioural aspects of faith mentioned in the previous section?

Vatican II (1962–65) marked a watershed in Catholicism in that the Church adopted a less defensive and more open attitude towards the world. Most previous Councils concluded their deliberations with a series of 'anathemas' or condemnations directed at opponents. Vatican II eschewed such an approach; it was a more pastoral Council, intent on affirming and encouraging Christians on their journey of faith.

Prior to Vatican II, faith was understood primarily in terms of obedience to revealed truths. Vatican I (1869–70) saw faith as a supernatural virtue by which, with the help of God, we believe that what God has revealed is true. Faith is seen as an affirmative act of the intellect. We believe not because of rational demonstration but because of the authority of God who reveals. Vatican I, therefore, emphasised faith as obedient assent to the doctrines which the Church teaches on God's authority. In this perspective faith tended to be equated with beliefs or doctrinal truths that can be formulated in propositions.

This important aspect of faith can be traced back to the beginnings of Christianity. In the New Testament we have short creedal statements, e.g. 'Jesus is Lord' (1 Cor 12:3; Rom 10:9), while the Creed we recite at Mass each Sunday has its origins in the fourth-century Councils of Nicea and Constantinople. In its *Constitution on Divine Revelation* (*Dei Verbum*) Vatican II affirmed this view of faith in terms of obedience to God who reveals, but it also went further. To make an act of faith requires grace or the help of the Holy Spirit, which turns the person towards God filling them with joy and giving them a deeper understanding of divine revelation (*Dei Verbum*, 5). In other words, faith is a wholehearted and personal response on the part of the believer to God's offer of salvation.

Vatican II developed a more personalist and biblically-informed notion of faith. The key article is *Dei Verbum*, 5 where faith is depicted as a free and trusting self-commitment to God who reveals, and as a willing and free assent to divinely revealed truth. Faith comes about both through proclamation or the preaching of the Gospel, and also by human inquiry and reasoning. The important point, as we have seen in the previous piece, is that faith involves a personal encounter and relationship with God mediated through the Church. One does not only go to God on one's own but in and with the believing community.

In his Apostolic Letter for the Year of Faith, *Porta Fidei* (2011), n. 10, Benedict XVI drew together these different strands of faith. He claimed that, 'there exists a profound unity between the act by which we believe and the content to which we give our assent' and he said that St Paul can help us

> enter into this reality when he writes: 'Man believes with his heart and so is justified, and he confesses with his lips and

so is saved' (Rom 10:10). The heart indicates that the first act by which one comes to faith is God's gift and the action of grace which acts and transforms the person deep within.

Benedict continued that a confession of faith 'with the lips indicates in turn that faith implies public testimony and commitment'. A Christian 'may never think of belief as a private act ... Profession of faith is an act both personal and communitarian'. At baptism the believer is incorporated into the faith of the Christian community as the way to salvation. Finally, Benedict pointed to the *Catechism of the Catholic Church* as an

> 'indispensable tool' to arrive at 'a systematic knowledge of the content of the faith ... On page after page, we find that what is presented here is no theory, but an encounter with a Person who lives within the Church' (*Porta Fidei*, 11).

In effect, Benedict is articulating the three dimensions of faith alluded to in the previous piece – the intellectual, the affective and the behavioural. The behavioural or practical dimension of faith was developed after Vatican II by Latin American theologians of liberation. Liberation theology, in contrast to more classical academic approaches, reflects on faith from 'the underside of history'. It is a way of doing theology which draws from the experiences of oppressed and suffering peoples. It is a protest at how theology had become detached from life. Hence liberation theology is a theology coming from the grass roots comprising social analysis of situations of injustice, which in turn leads to liberating action. If the goal of classical theology was to *understand* the faith, the goal of liberation theology includes the aim of *changing* the unjust situation. The Bible is seen as a source of empowerment and liberation in this process. Although aspects of the methodology of liberation theology have been criticised, it has vividly highlighted how all theology must be contextual and practical. The understanding of faith and the pursuit of justice and truth are of a piece.

10

How do Christians understand faith in other religions?

Declan Marmion

What are Christians to make of other religions? Are they also ways of salvation for their adherents? And has the Church changed its attitude towards non-Christian religions over the years?

Christianity has not always valued dialogue with other religions. Theological assessments of other religions tended, on the whole, to be negative and this trend persisted into the twentieth century. Little positive was said about the possible role of other religions in God's plan. The tendency was to repress difference and to dismiss other religions as heresies. Truth and grace in other faiths were, at most, 'stepping stones' superseded by Christian revelation.

The motto 'outside the Church, no salvation,' originally linked with Cyprian of Carthage (d.258), has been an oft-repeated refrain through the centuries. Non-Christians, it seemed, had little hope of salvation. For example, there was the statement of the Council of Florence (1442) that 'all those who are outside the Catholic Church, not only pagans but Jews or heretics and schismatics, cannot share in eternal life and will go *into the everlasting fire which was prepared for the devil and his angels*' (Mt 25:41). While the phrase, 'outside the Church, no salvation' encapsulated traditional thinking about the position of unbelievers, there were other strands of Catholic theological thinking that were less pessimistic. One example is Thomas Aquinas who spoke about how one can be saved through a 'baptism by desire' in the absence of actual baptism. People could be seen as being part of the Church through baptism *in re* (in reality) or *in voto* (in desire). The Council of Trent (1542) also referred to this distinction, stating that transition to the state of grace 'cannot take place without the waters of rebirth or the desire for them'. And more recently we have the reassuring affirmation of the International Theological Commission that 'the Church has never once declared the damnation of a single person as a concrete fact' (International Theological Commission, 'Some Current Questions in Eschatology' [1992], 10.3).

It was at Vatican II that a more positive stance of openness, dialogue and appreciation of other faiths developed. The new attitude of the Council towards other religions needs to be seen against the backdrop of its openness to the world at large and its emphasis on the universal salvific will of God, which contrasted with previous, more rigid, attitudes towards non-Christians. Vatican II spoke of 'all people of good will in whose hearts grace is active invisibly' (*Gaudium et spes*, 22; see also *Lumen Gentium*, 16). The Council wanted to affirm the positive values enshrined in other religious traditions and cultures. They contain 'elements of truth and grace' (*Ad Gentes*, 9), 'seeds of the Word' (*AG*, 11, 15) and fruits of the Spirit. The Spirit of God is seen as at work in other religions not only in their religious aspirations but also in the human values they pursue – including justice, harmony and peace.

As Vatican II's *Declaration on the Relation of the Church to Non-Christian Religions* (*Nostra Aetate*, 2) put it:

> The Catholic Church rejects nothing that is true and holy
> in these religions. She regards with sincere reverence those
> ways of conduct and of life, those precepts and teachings
> which, though differing in many aspects from the ones she
> holds and sets forth, nonetheless often reflect a ray of that
> Truth which enlightens all men. Indeed, she proclaims, and
> ever must proclaim Christ 'the way, the truth, and the life'
> (Jn 14:6), in whom men may find the fullness of religious
> life, in whom God has reconciled all things to Himself.

The documents of Vatican II, therefore, tried to incorporate
the possible salvation not only of Christians but also of non-
Christians. The Council affirmed those who were still
searching, or who have not had the Gospel preached to
them, as well as non-Christians living upright lives:

> There are those who without any fault do not know any-
> thing about Christ or his Church, yet who search for God
> with a sincere heart and, under the influence of grace, try
> to put into effect the will of God as known to them through
> the dictate of conscience: these too can obtain eternal sal-
> vation (*LG*, 16).

Moreover, the Council believed that the Holy Spirit continues to blow where it wills (Jn 3:8) actively bringing about
God's purpose for humanity:

> Since Christ died for everyone, and since the ultimate call-
> ing of each of us comes from God and is therefore a univer-
> sal one, we are obliged to hold that the Holy Spirit offers
> everyone the possibility of sharing in this paschal mystery
> in a manner known to God (*GS*, 22).

A Christian faith that takes religious plurality seriously
needs to maintain the 'uniqueness' and 'universality' of
Jesus Christ as saviour, but not in a way that excludes the
possibility of non-Christians being saved. As John Paul II
put it in his first encyclical *Redemptor hominis* (1979) the Fathers at Vatican II

rightly saw in the various religions as it were so many reflections of the one truth, 'seeds of the Word' attesting that, though the routes taken may be different, there is but a single goal to which is directed the deepest aspiration of the human spirit as expressed in its quest for God (n. 11).

In other words, salvation reaches men and women in and through their own religions, not in spite of them. These are expressions of the human openness to God and signs of God's presence in the world.

11

What is the Doctrine of Mary's Immaculate Conception about?

Brendan Leahy

In the lead-up to Christmas every year the Catholic Church celebrates the Feast Day of the Immaculate Conception. Sometimes it's not clear what exactly we are celebrating. Is it the same as the doctrine of Mary's virginity? Some people interpret it as a statement that sex is bad. What does it mean to say that Mary was 'immaculate'?

It's true that the Immaculate Conception sometimes gets confused with other aspects of our faith. Mary's virginity, for instance, is about her conceiving Jesus in her womb by the power of the Holy Spirit rather than as a result of a sexual union with a man. Jesus has only one Father – God the Father. His relationship with the Father is a central theme of the Gospels. The doctrine of the Immaculate Conception, on the other hand, is about Mary's own identity from the first moment of her existence – she was totally sinless, open to God. This is not a statement about how Mary was conceived. She was conceived in the normal way through the sexual union of her parents, Joachim and Anna.

Often Mary's preservation from original sin sounds negative. But it can and should also be thought of positively.

Original sin is not to be confused with our personal sins. Original sin is more about a deep-rooted turning against God that is written into history, into our social environment and into our lives. We are born into it. We find ourselves touched by this turn against God and so we need salvation, redemption and freedom in order to be able to turn in love towards God and one another. Only God can free us.

When God, who is Love, wanted to enter this world in order to bring us to share in his life and set us free, he needed an access point in history where he would be perfectly accepted and welcomed. This is the context for understanding Mary's Immaculate Conception. Being preserved from original sin meant she was full of grace, full of love and so able at the Annunciation to perfectly welcome without any obstacles whatever the fullness of God-Love come among us in Jesus Christ.

It might seem that Mary's Immaculate Conception removes her from us – she's too perfect, too spotless. But in fact the opposite is the case. It is precisely because she is so full of love that she also knew more than all others the extent to which sin and division impact on people. Love gives eyes and a heart to know what others are going through. Mary understood and was in solidarity more than anyone else with suffering humanity.

The doctrine of the Immaculate Conception is, therefore, a hopeful teaching. It tells us that at the heart of the Church we have a point where God-Love has been perfectly loved and we are embraced within that. No matter how imperfect our 'yes' to God who has come among us in Jesus Christ may be, it can be uttered as an echo of Mary's immaculate 'yes'.

From earliest times, certainly in the second century, reference was made to Mary's miraculous conception. The Church came to understand her Immaculate Conception by reading, living and re-reading the Scriptures. St Paul, for instance, writes how we are all called to be 'immaculate'. It seems that perhaps firstly in Ireland but then certainly in England a feast celebrating Mary's conception began already around 1000.

There were difficulties in understanding the doctrine. Theologians, especially in the twelfth and thirteenth centuries, faced a conundrum. They knew Mary was uniquely holy, special, worthy of veneration but since it is our faith that Jesus Christ is the saviour of all humankind, how can Mary be exempt? She too needs to be saved, does she not? So how could she be immaculate from her conception before Christ?

It was the Franciscan theologian, Duns Scotus, who offered a simple solution that helped. He made the point that yes, all of us need to be saved by Jesus Christ. And that is true of Mary too. But in her case, God applied to her in advance the salvation that would come into humanity through Jesus' death and resurrection. He did so in view of the unique mission she was to carry out as the Mother of God.

On 8 December, 1854 Pope Pius IX declared to be infallible the doctrine that holds that

> the most Blessed Virgin Mary, in the first instance of her conception, by a singular grace and privilege granted by Almighty God, in view of the merits of Jesus Christ, the Saviour of the human race, was preserved free from all stain of original sin.

The Pope had previously consulted the bishops of the world to see if this doctrine was in accordance with what Catholics believed. Their answer was a resounding 'yes'.

One final point. Mary was immaculate by a gift from the Triune God of Love from the first moment of her conception. But in baptism we too are given the gift of an immaculate new start in life (freed from original sin)! The Christian life then is a journey of letting that gift have an effect in our lives; of letting ourselves become immaculate, that is, full of love. We have been chosen in Christ before the foundation of the world 'to be holy and blameless ... in love ...' (Eph 1:3–5). It's good to be reminded of this before Christmas as we celebrate Mary's Immaculate Conception.

12

Did Jesus have faith?

Brendan Leahy

Christians affirm they believe in Jesus Christ, the Word made flesh, the Son of God, 'true God from true God' as the Creed puts it. They also look to Jesus as an example, a model in so many ways. But can we say that Jesus is a model for us in our own journey of faith? Did he have faith?

The first preaching of the Apostles centred on Jesus Christ as Lord. He was the One the first Christians believed to be risen from the dead. They believed in him as Saviour of the world. In that sense, Jesus was the 'object' of their faith. But still the question could be asked: in his earthly existence, did Jesus himself have faith? In the third part of the *Summa Theologiae*, question 7, article 3, Thomas Aquinas explored this question and his conclusion, in itself very rich and nuanced, was negative: Jesus did not have the theological virtue of faith. He had a clear, beatific, vision of God.

It's true that the Fourth Gospel, for instance, speaks of Jesus' vision of the Father: 'Not that anyone has seen the Father except the one who is from God; he has seen the Father' (Jn 6:46; cf., Jn 1:18). The unique and intimate, direct and immediate vision and knowledge that Jesus had of the Father certainly rules out any question of Jesus, the Son of God, having faith in the sense of believing what he did not see.

Nevertheless, in Heb 12:2 we are encouraged to look 'to Jesus the pioneer and perfecter of our faith'. This seems to indicate that Jesus can be a model for Christians in their faith relationship with God. In what sense?

In the Old Testament, faith was viewed as a personal, trusting surrender to God who is always faithful to the Covenant. Abraham was the great model of this. Jesus, born a Jew, fulfils the faith of Abraham. A review of the Gospels indicates that Jesus' whole life was an extended act of trust and self-giving to the One he called 'Abba, Father'. In the Fourth Gospel we are told how Jesus described his 'food' as doing the will of him who sent him to complete his work (Jn 4:34). He was constantly open and trusting, self-surrendering and obedient as Son to God the Father.

But Jesus' obedience, in the power of the Spirit, to the Father involved active and free choice. He had to make everyday decisions, work out what steps to take in life, how to remain on course in carrying out the mission he was sent to do. He did so within the unique relationship he had, in the Holy Spirit, with the Father. He only 'knew' as much as God the Father willed him to know.

Where we see Jesus' total and radical fidelity to the Father is above all in his death on the Cross. Jesus even reached the point of crying out 'why' on the Cross (Mk 27:46; Mk 15:34). He no longer 'knew'. And yet, despite everything, as Luke's Gospel shows us, Jesus lived out his trust in the Father. It is in this sense that Jesus is the supreme model of faith. He is faithful in love of God always, even in the face of limits, darkness and absurdity, adversity and contradiction. Jesus only wants to know what God the Father's will is for him. And this trust was confirmed by the Father in the Resurrection.

While, as the Son of God, Jesus' experience is unique (and therefore his faith is not to be reduced simply to our faith) nevertheless he is a model for Christians who are called to live out the attitude of faith he has shown us. In living out our faith as self-surrendering trust in God the Father we are not simply *imitating* Jesus. Something great has happened because of Jesus' life, death and resurrection. Through the gift of baptism, Christians are given the possibility of *participating* personally and together in Jesus' faith in the sense that we are incorporated into Christ in his relationship with God the Father.

Sharing in Jesus' life, Christians are called to live out the same dynamic of free response, in the Spirit, to God the Father who has loved us first. The more we have faith, the more we will 'see' God's will. Our adherence to the *contents* of Christian faith is always to be accompanied by our *act* of faith in the sense of trusting in God, letting ourselves be taken up into the new divine life that is nothing less than a sharing in the life of the Trinity. We are to make our own the new criterion of intelligence that has opened up for us in Christ. As St Paul puts it, 'The life I now live in the flesh I live by faith in the Son of God' and 'It is no longer I who live, but Christ who lives in me' (Gal 2:20).

One final point. Christian faith is uniquely personal to each one of us. But it is never a private, individual-centred vertical relationship with God. We go to God together. In this sense faith is ecclesial precisely because we have been made 'one' in Christ, sons and daughters in the Son. Our faith unites us in Christ: 'for in Christ Jesus you are all children of God through faith. As many of you as were baptised into Christ have clothed yourselves with Christ' (Gal 3:26–27). Our 'faith works through love' (Gal 5:6), especially love of one another. Participating together in Christ's faith we 'do' the truth in love (Eph 4:15) and this brings about unity among us in Christ 'so that the world will believe' (Jn 17:21).

13

What or Who is the Kingdom of God?

Brendan Leahy

The expression 'the Kingdom (of heaven) of God' is found 122 times in the New Testament and we find Jesus speaking of it in the Gospels no less than 69 times. In the past century there has been a rediscovery that the Kingdom was at the heart of Jesus' preaching. But what is the 'Kingdom of God'?

A well-known Scripture scholar I knew in America told me how he was amazed that after many years of saying Mass every Sunday in the same parish, on one particular Sunday on which he preached on the Kingdom of God, someone commented to him afterwards that it was the first time they had ever heard of that.

And yet, to be a Christian is to be someone who is bringing forward the Kingdom of God! As the German theologian, Jürgen Moltmann, has written: 'anyone who gets involved with Jesus gets involved with the Kingdom of God'.

In the Gospels Jesus doesn't provide a crisp neat definition of the Kingdom. Rather his method to get across his message about the Kingdom was more 'come and see'. In Matthew's Gospel, for instance, we are told that when John the Baptist heard in prison what Jesus was doing, he sent word by his disciples to ask him: 'Are you the one who is to come, or are we to wait for another?' Jesus answered them: 'Go and tell John what you hear and see: the blind receive their sight, the lame walk, the lepers are cleansed, the deaf hear, the dead are raised, and the poor have good news brought to them' (Mt 11:2–6; see also Luke's description of Jesus' personal mission statement: Lk 4:16–20).

The Kingdom of God was 'happening' wherever Jesus went. In encountering him, people turned around towards God in a new way and they began to see one another with new eyes. People discovered the mercy of God and they began to form relationships of mutual love, forgiveness and reconciliation, justice and truth. They joined the new community that was coming to life around Jesus. They went out to others with the 'Good News'. We see it, for instance, in the conversation between Jesus and the Samaritan woman at Jacob's well (see Jn 4).

Jesus is clear that we shouldn't confuse the Kingdom with kingdoms of this world or simply earthly progress. It is of a different nature. As St Paul affirms: 'the kingdom of God is not food and drink but righteousness and peace and joy in the Holy Spirit' (Rom 14:17).

We could summarise it as follows. The Kingdom of God is an event of the personal and merciful, liberating and holy God making himself present in this world in and through Jesus. The Kingdom 'happens' today too. Drawn by the Holy Spirit we come to know Jesus Christ. This changes our whole life. It is firstly an interior event, an inner realisation that God loves me immensely. My response to this is to put God in the first place in my life over all others things, people and myself. The Church Father, Origen, in his treatise 'On Prayer', commenting on this dimension of the Kingdom could write: 'Then let God stroll at leisure in us as in a spiritual paradise.'[1]

---

[1] See 'On Prayer' in *Patrologia Graeca*, 11, p. 495ff as quoted in Pope Benedict XVI, *Jesus of Nazareth*, p. 50.

While our encounter with and entrance into the Kingdom is deeply personal, it becomes manifest in changed relationships. Jesus Christ reaches us in and through the preaching of the Word and the community life of the Church. We enter the Church as the place where the Kingdom of God can be experienced. (Catholics look to the episode in the Gospels when Jesus said to Peter: 'I will give you the keys of the kingdom of heaven, and whatever you bind on earth will be bound in heaven, and whatever you loose on earth will be loosed in heaven.' Mt 16:19)

We can really say we've 'entered' the Kingdom of God when we are living the Gospel in our everyday life. We bring forward the Kingdom of God when we offer forgiveness and build up relationships of reconciliation and unity, truth and justice, mercy and love.

The Church itself in its visible boundaries cannot be identified with the Kingdom (as perhaps there was a tendency to do in the past) but rather as a seed and beginning of the Kingdom. The Kingdom will only be fully fulfilled at the end of time. Now, within history, in and through the Church as a community of Word and sacrament, ministry, charism and love, Jesus, in the power of the Spirit, is gathering his family into the Kingdom.

In the Gospel we read of the image of the seed sown in the soil that grows up to become a large tree. So it is with the Kingdom of God. Cast into the furrows of history, it is growing steadily. Perhaps we cannot always see its growth or easily describe it. But in faith we know the tree will one day be fully blossoming.

14

How are we to interpret Jesus' 'why' question on the Cross?

Brendan Leahy

It is quite remarkable that in both Matthew and Mark's Gospel the only word that we hear Jesus utter on the Cross is a question: 'my God, my God, why have you forsaken me?' What are we to make of this cry – a desperate and haunting plea at the end of a failed mission? A despairing search for answers in the face of overwhelming doubt?

There's something almost embarrassing for Christians that Jesus' cry at the end of his life seems to indicate he no longer felt God's presence. He had spent his whole life proclaiming the closeness of the loving and merciful, liberating and holy God that he called 'Abba', Father.

Firstly, it should be noted that in writing up their account of Jesus' passion, the evangelists made ample use of Ps 22. That psalm opens with the line 'why have you forsaken me?' So Jesus' 'why' question can be understood as simply referring to the prayer he recited while dying. If we read the whole psalm we realise it is a prayer of ultimate trust in God's victory over death: 'To you they cried, and were saved; in you they trusted, and were not put to shame … Do not be far from me, for trouble is near and there is no one to help' (Ps 22:5, 11). So it is not the cry of a man without hope but rather of infinite trust. Luke brings out this trusting aspect of Jesus on the Cross when he tells us of Jesus continuing to love in imploring forgiveness for his executioners.

And yet spiritual writers and scholars also point out today that it is important to recognise that Jesus' 'why' question might not simply have been a prayer. When Mark and Matthew included it, they wanted to remind us of the real suffering and darkness Jesus was going through on the Cross. Jesus is both human and divine. It would be perfectly understandable that Jesus who was like us in all things but sin should suffer dreadful anguish when we consider how utterly abandoned he was by the political and religious authorities of the time and even by his own disciples. A careful study of how Mark constructed his account of Jesus' passion indicates that he used various sentences of Ps 22 in such a way as to bring out how Jesus was increasingly isolated in the last days and hours of his earthly life.

In the Old Testament Book of Deuteronomy (21:23) we read that those who died on the Cross were to be considered excluded from the Covenant people. For Jesus to die on the Cross must have seemed to many as his exclusion from the Covenant people. Jesus' cry was the cry of all who are excluded. He had made his own the pain of all forms of abandonment. St Paul develops this point in a set of paradoxes that he often repeats. Jesus is excluded in order to include us in his relationship with the Father. He is weak in order to make us strong. He is poor to make us rich. He is cursed to bring us blessing. His *cry* is to be the reply to our *'whys'*.

In this light, then, Jesus' cry on the Cross tells us how much God loves us. He sent his Son to enter right into the depths of our human condition, reaching even its limit point of feeling distance from God and passing into death. It is from within this experience that Jesus, in his divine humanity, entered into the Resurrection.

In making his own all the negativity we can experience, Jesus transformed everything from within. He made of our darkness and fragility, emptiness and poverty the very place where he is now to be found. Jesus' 'why' question on the Cross tells us there is no situation of desolation, despair or doubt where we cannot find the presence of Jesus who says,

> I have experienced your wound; I too have cried out 'why'; I am the One who laid down my life for you; I am here in this situation; imitate me in keeping on trusting and loving.

15

What is meant by saying that Christ 'descended into hell'?

Martin Henry

In the Apostles' Creed, after the reference to the death and burial of Christ, we read that 'he descended into hell'. What is actually meant by this assertion?

The credal statement of Christ's descent into hell is quite startling, when one begins to reflect on it in any depth. For hell is regarded – at any rate in popular imagination – as the final destination for those who have definitively rejected God's will and his love for humanity. Hence, one would inevitably wonder how Christ, who did the Father's will in season and out of season, and, in his passion and crucifixion, offered his life to the Father rather than trying to save it by any means at his disposal, could have found himself after death in the situation of those who had entirely rejected God. This seems a blatantly preposterous state of affairs.

The classical doctrine of hell has been a staple element of church teaching over the centuries, constantly overshadowing the more upbeat expressions of hope for humanity's eschatological or ultimate prospects associated with theologians like the great Alexandrian thinker Origen, in the early church, and the Swiss writer Hans Urs von Balthasar, in the twentieth century. Official church teaching on hell was ratified by the Council of Florence in the fifteenth century, and the Council of Trent in the sixteenth, and incorporated into the *Catechism of the Catholic Church* (par. 1035) in 1994. But clearly the term 'hell' in Christ's 'descent into hell' cannot be interpreted as referring to the church's traditional understanding of hell as the state of eternal damnation or separation from God.

The notion itself of Christ's descent into hell does, however, have a foothold in the New Testament in the letters of St Paul (Rom 10:7; Eph 4:8–10) and 1 Pet (3:19–20; 4:6). And perhaps faint echoes of the notion can be heard in Mt 27:52–54 and Lk 23:43. The theme of Christ's descent into hell was particularly developed in the Eastern Christian tradition:

> Icons, wall-paintings, and mosaics of the Anastasis [resurrection] show Christ trampling on the Gates of Hell, driving out devils, and reaching for the hand of Adam, who, with Eve and the Patriarchs, is rescued from the underworld (Peter and Linda Murray, *The Oxford Companion to Christian Art and Architecture*, p. 15).

In medieval English mystery plays, this was to become the theme of Christ's 'Harrowing of Hell'.

Christ's descent into hell refers, therefore, not to 'hell' in the traditional sense, but to the ancient Christian belief that Christ preached the good news of salvation to the just of the Old Testament who had lived before he came, and were waiting in the underworld for their redemption. It has little or nothing to do with what came to be the classical notion of hell as the place of eternal punishment of the damned, a place or condition of unending distress and despair. 'Harrowing', in the English expression: the 'Harrowing of Hell', does not refer to anguish or suffering of any kind, but has rather the meaning of 'robbing', as if Christ had made a kind of triumphant 'smash-and-grab' raid on the abode of the devil, overpowered or outwitted him, and rescued those who had been waiting for him.

It is, however, important to mention another modern interpretation of Christ's 'descent into hell' that has been quite influential in recent decades. This is the interpretation of the belief to be found in the writings of the Swiss theologian referred to above, von Balthasar. The latter interprets the descent into hell in a quasi-Lutheran way as referring to Christ's experience of complete abandonment by, or separation from, God in death before overcoming the total anguish of such alienation in the Resurrection. Balthasar's mystical associate, Adrienne von Speyr, is also closely linked with the promotion of this idea. Yet it appears to be a highly-speculative interpretation of the statement in the creed and does not seem to rest on any very precise evidence. By way of comparison, it is interesting to note briefly how, in an earlier age, the Reformer John Calvin interpreted the article of the creed that is at issue. Calvin had a quite no-nonsense interpretation of the matter:

> For Calvin, the affirmation that the Christ had really gone down into hell after his death belonged to the domain of fables; the descent into hell ought to be regarded simply as an image for the sufferings endured by Christ on the cross and of his death in the flesh (François Wendel, *Calvin: The Origins and Development of his Religious Thought*, pp. 82–3).

A more sinister interpretation of Christ's descent into hell, on the other hand, is attributed to the second-century heretic, Marcion, who is reported to have seen in it an argument against the credibility of the Catholic understanding of God's mercy. According to the Romanian writer, Emile Cioran (*Aveux et Anathèmes*, p. 9), Marcion portrayed the just of the Old Testament period as being suspicious of

Christ's message of liberation and refusing to budge, whereas Cain and his ilk immediately seized their chance and left hell with Christ. For the just, in Marcion's theology, the good news was too good to be true; it couldn't apply to the tribe of Cain.

The enduring significance of the creed's statement on hell lies in its claim that the redemption won by Christ is for all human beings, both those who lived before and those who live after Christ. Christianity is, in short, catholic.

16

What does it mean to say Jesus rose from the dead?

Brendan Leahy

In the Gospels we read that during his life Jesus raised Lazarus and the daughter of Jairus from the dead. What was his own Resurrection like? What difference does Jesus' Resurrection make in our lives?

Looking simply in terms of cause and effect, the hiatus between the end of Jesus' life with the shameful event of the Crucifixion and the early explosion into life of the Christian movement is hard to explain. His scandalous death doesn't tally with the new enthusiastic faith of the early Christians. As the nineteenth century rationalist David Strauss put it, the formidable turnaround from the profound depression and total desperation caused by the death of Jesus to the enthusiasm with which the disciples announced Jesus as Messiah cannot be explained unless in the meantime some exceptionally encouraging event occurred. Christians affirm this event was the Resurrection. Central to Christianity is the affirmation that 'Jesus is risen!'.

In one of his Letters, St Paul states clearly: 'If Christ has not been raised, then our proclamation has been in vain and your faith has been in vain ... If Christ has not been raised, your faith is futile and you are still in your sins' (1 Cor 15:14, 17). It has been the conviction of Christians through the centuries. The Churches of the East, for instance, offer each other an Easter greeting after the Easter ceremonies: '*Christos anesti* – Christ is risen!' and the response: '*Aleithos Anesti* – Yes, he is truly risen'.

The main source of belief in Jesus' Resurrection from the dead is the Resurrection appearances and the empty tomb. The way the appearances are narrated in the New Testament indicates they weren't some form of hallucination or people projecting an image. Nor were they simply a case of resuscitation. Lazarus and the daughter of Jairus were raised up in the sense of resuscitation. They would die again. Resurrection in the case of Jesus is much, much more.

In the Resurrection Jesus enters a new realm of existence. He now shares fully in God's glory. He is now beyond the limitations of space and time that he experienced in his earthly life. In the power of the Spirit he is now universally present to everyone and everywhere. He is now thoroughly available to everyone, encounterable in faith and in the Spirit. In this sense, the Risen Christ precedes the Church's missionary efforts to witness explicitly to the good news.

The empty tomb in itself is not definite proof of the Resurrection but it does back up the basic belief that it isn't that Jesus simply rose in some spiritual sense or in terms of living on in people's memory. Emphasising the empty tomb, the Evangelists want to remind us that Jesus' *whole* existence has entered into the new realm of sharing fully in God's life. A human heart now beats in God. And our bodily and concrete existence, our human history, has been touched by the Resurrection.

Benedict XVI, Pope emeritus, has written that the Resurrection is the qualitative leap that humanity and creation have been waiting for. He calls it the last and highest 'evolutionary leap', the union of the finite with the infinite, the union of humanity and God, the conquest of death. Christ's risen and transformed body has now become 'the place' where people enter into communion with God and with one another and are so able to live in the fullness of a life that will never end. St Paul often wrote of how we live 'in Christ' and 'in the Spirit'. Or again in the words of the Acts of the Apostles, 'in him we live and move and have our being'.

How is the Risen Jesus present in and to this world? He is present in his reconciling and uniting outreach. As the Second Eucharistic Prayer of Reconciliation affirms, 'By the working of your power it comes about, O Lord, that hatred is overcome by love, revenge gives way to forgiveness, and discord is changed to mutual respect.'

The Risen Christ is present to us in many ways – he speaks to us through his Word preached, contemplated and lived. He is present in the poor as we read in Mt 25 ('whatever you do to the least you do to me'). He is present in those who succeed to the apostles – the bishops and priests ('he who hears you hears me' [Lk 10:16]). He is present especially in the Eucharist ('I am the Bread of Life … come down from heaven' [Jn 6:51]). Today we are particularly sensitive to his continuing presence in the Church, not only in its institutional structures of sustaining and building up holiness (sacraments, the hierarchy), but also 'where two or three are gathered' in his name (Mt 18:20) because he promised: 'I will be with you to the end of the ages' (Mt 28:20). It is in mutual love, reconciliation and love of enemy that his Risen presence becomes more tangible and 'visible'.

Christian hope is that after our death we too will share fully in the new eternal life that has opened up in Jesus' death and resurrection. Already now in faith and love, every time we pass from death to life in loving our neighbour we begin to experience something of the life and light of the Resurrection.

17

What is the point of the Ascension?

Martin Henry

It is sometimes thought that the Resurrection and the Ascension are simply two terms for the one reality, namely Christ's conquest of death. However, the Creed appears to distinguish between them. So, if the Resurrection means rising from the dead, to what does the Ascension refer?

The opening of the Acts of the Apostles reports that Jesus appeared to his disciples for forty days after his Resurrection and then ascended into heaven, leaving the disciples somewhat at a loss about what to do next. From our vantage point, we know that what happened next was that the disciples received the Holy Spirit at Pentecost and went out into the whole world to preach the gospel to all the nations.

However, it's still helpful for us today to look back to the Ascension and to remind ourselves about what it in essence means. It certainly signalled the beginning of the church's history, but it also indicates the destiny to which humanity is called. Hence while it's important to keep in mind that Jesus rose from the dead, it's just as important to recall what happened when Jesus rose from the dead. Or perhaps in order to see what's really involved here, it might be better to ask: 'For what purpose did Jesus rise from the dead?'

And that's what the Ascension can tell us. Because the Ascension shows that Jesus rose from the dead so as to return to his Father in Heaven. And we too hope to rise from the dead, not just so as to be able to say we have survived death, but in order to reach Heaven and to be with God and to live the fullness of life with God and all those who have gone before us into eternity, 'with the sign of faith'.

In short, it's why we want to rise from the dead that should really concern us, not just whether we are going to survive death or not. At his brother's burial, St Ambrose said that eternal life would be just a weariness – or, we might say, 'a bore' – were it not transfigured by grace. Perhaps this is what the German philosopher Nietzsche was provocatively hinting at when he contrasted 'eternal life' with *'eternal liveliness'*.

Yet it would be disingenuous to ignore the fact that in modern times the link between life on earth and, for Christian faith, its final glorious denouement in Heaven, has become not so much difficult to perceive, but has, rather, been rejected, not to say resented, as a pernicious threat to living authentically on earth. The hope of Heaven is frequently seen as undermining the possibility of living life with maximum honesty and intensity. The Nietzsche admirer and commentator, Walter Kaufmann, may be taken as a fairly characteristic representative of such a modern attitude. In his *The Faith of a Heretic,* he writes unapologetically:

> The life I want is a life I could not endure in eternity. It is a
> life of love and intensity, suffering and creation, that makes
> life worthwhile and death welcome. There is no other life
> I should prefer. Neither should I like not to die.

This is no doubt a salutary warning about the dangers of speaking too glibly about eternal life. And it might help us to realize that what most concerns us, or at least ought to concern us, about eternal life, should be the *quality* of that eternal life. In short, what should most matter to us is not whether there is an eternal life or not, but rather whether our eternity is going to be a life of joy and happiness with God and each other, or whether it is going to be an eternity of gloom and despondency. This presumably is what the church's teaching about heaven and hell is trying to point up.

Not everyone agrees with Christian faith on this particular point, of course. Quite apart from those who, like Walter Kaufmann, find any idea of eternal life not only meaningless but potentially inimical to the business of living *this* life, one could point to the very *sui generis* attitude to the possibility of hell of the Spanish religious thinker, Miguel de Unamuno, who wrote that he would rather spend eternity in hell, than cease to exist altogether. That is certainly an unusual and, if not life-affirming, at least self-affirming, point of view. And it differs, interestingly enough, from both orthodox Christianity and the convictions of a thinker like Walter Kaufmann, at least in formulation.

But traditionally, what Christianity has taught is that the deepest truth there is, is not simply the fact of our own existence, but rather God himself, and the belief that God wishes to share his life with us. Hence the importance of the Ascension. It is not just a reinforcement of belief in the Resurrection, but it celebrates the reason for wanting to rise from the dead, which for Christian faith is to be able to share in God's own life for all eternity.

Curiously enough, even paradoxically, on this very point Christian belief does seem to find a distinct, if fairly distant echo in Nietzsche's famous lines, placed in the mouth of Zarathustra in his work, *Thus Spoke Zarathustra* (Penguin Edition, p. 333):

> The world is deep,
> Deeper than day can comprehend.
> Deep is its woe,
> Joy – deeper than heart's agony:
> Woe says: Fade! Go!
> But all joy wants eternity,
> Wants deep, deep, deep eternity!
>
> (Trans. R.J. Hollingdale)

18

What is the role of the Holy Spirit in our lives?

Mary McCaughey

Christianity is about following Jesus Christ by living the golden rule, 'love God ... and love your neighbor as yourself' (Lk 10:27). What does the Holy Spirit have to do with following Christ? Did the Holy Spirit not just come once and for all at Pentecost to empower the early Church to preach the Gospel? Or is the Holy Spirit the love between the Father and the Son in the inner life of the Trinity? What has the Spirit got to do with our lives?

The Holy Spirit in fact has a lot to do with us, the life of the Church today and how we live our Christian life! The Spirit is the power and strength of God given to us so that our Christian faith is always alive and life-giving to us and others. As Jesus said in conversation with the woman from Samaria by the well of Jacob and says today to us: 'If only you knew the gift of God' (Jn 4:10).

To understand the role of the Holy Spirit in our lives, we need to understand God's relationship with us. God creates human beings in his image and likeness (Gen 1:24), but doesn't then abandon us. Jesus Christ, the perfect image of God (2 Cor 4:4; Col 1:15; Heb 1:3) is *the* son of God. While Christ is the Son of God by nature through the Holy Spirit we now become adopted children of the Father. The Holy

Spirit, the love which unites Christ and the Father is now poured into each of our hearts (Rom 5:5) and we too now relate to God as our 'Abba' (Rom 8:14). Through the Spirit each of us is constantly being recreated and moulded lovingly into the image of Christ within the life of the Church particularly through Word and Sacrament.

On Christ the Messiah rests 'the Spirit of the Lord ... the spirit of wisdom and understanding, the spirit of counsel and might, the spirit of knowledge and the fear of the Lord' (Isa 11:2). After Christ's death and ascent to the Father, the Spirit is breathed out and descends on his Body, at Pentecost. Yet there was not simply a once and for all historical descent of the Spirit on the Church. The Church is now the messianic community who lives the life of Christ today in the power of the Holy Spirit on its pilgrim journey through this world. Following on from Baptism, the gift of the Holy Spirit given at Confirmation prepares the People of God to be 'prophets,' and witness publically to God in the world. Like Christ the Messiah, they are called to proclaim freedom to those who are enslaved to a life and separation from God and from others (Lk 4:18). The Spirit prays in the baptised 'with sighs too deep for human words' (Rom 8:26) enabling them to worship in 'Spirit and Truth' (John 4:24) rather than simply as an external ritual. The charisms of the Spirit such as the gifts of teaching, prophecy and healing (1 Cor 12:1–13), build up Church communities and yet the ultimate charism is charity: God's own love in us (1 Cor 13) expressed in unity.

Life according to the Holy Spirit does not mean being 'otherworldly'. It is a way of life rooted in Christ's Incarnation and our dignity as embodied human beings. Rather life in the Spirit leads us towards others and towards action in the world. It is not about legal minimalism but of fullness according to the new law 'written upon our hearts'. Living this new law is to live according to the Beatitudes (Mt 5) of which Christ is the model. It is the life of the new creature in the Church, seen in Mary the spouse of the Holy Spirit. It is expressed in 'purity in heart,' putting God first and seeing the world from God's perspective (faith); 'poverty of Spirit,' depending on God alone, rather than material possessions; in 'peacemaking,' building unity through a spirit of reconciliation and courage in acceptance of misunderstanding for living this way of truth in the Spirit.

It is the Holy Spirit who continually keeps the Church alive in Christ. The Church's task is not simply to hand on a historical set of beliefs, sayings and commandments given by Christ and the Christian community at a point in history. Rather it is the Spirit who keeps the Word of God alive and active in the Church *today* to change our lives. It is through the Spirit that the sacraments can really unite us *today* to Christ in his risen life. To live in the Spirit is to live a life of freedom by the power and grace of God. It is a gift for living Christian faith amidst life's ups and downs and to become each day anew more like Christ, who is by nature what we are by adoption – a child of the Father. Through the presence of the Holy Spirit in our lives, God's promise is fulfilled: 'I will not leave you orphans' (Jn 14:18) and 'I am with you until the end of the age' (Mt 28:20).

19

What are we to make of statements such as 'I believe in God but not in the Church!'?

Noel O'Sullivan

Some people articulate their difficulties with faith as having to do with the Church but not with God: 'I have great faith in God and Our Lady; I go to the local church to light a candle but don't ask me to go to Mass; the Church does nothing for me.'

One-Sided View of Church

All too often we only hear of the human and fragile side of the Church but the Church is not simply an institution made up of human beings. The Church is both a human institution and a spiritual reality, the Body of Christ. When people walk away from the Church it is often the case that they have been put off by the human failings of the institution. Their disappointment is understandable but it is such a pity to cut oneself off from the wonderful spiritual resource that is also the Church. The French Dominican, Yves Congar, drew an interesting parallel between the Church and Christ. Just as there are two natures in Christ we can speak of two elements in the Church: the human and the divine. In the case of the Church the human side can fail and be sinful. This is not so of course with the humanity of Christ. The parallel between the two natures in Christ and the two elements in the Church, human and divine, helps us to distinguish between the failures of the Church, on the one hand, and the divine side of the Church, on the other. The Church is the Body of Christ: it is a spiritual reality that will not be destroyed. Just before he left us Jesus said: 'And remember, I am with you always, to the end of the age' (Mt 28:20).

Individualism versus Community

Another factor that causes difficulty with the Church is a rabid individualism. Some people find the idea of community distasteful. They want to come to God on their own and not as part of a community. But Christianity is of its nature communitarian or social. This has its origin in God himself: God is not an isolated individual but a community of love. Though there is only one God, this God is made up of three persons. The ultimate goal of being a Christian is to enter the life of the Trinity, to be caught up in its inner movement. We make this journey with other people, not in splendid isolation.

Old Testament Roots

The Church is in continuity with the *qahal*, the assembly of the Old Testament, a term translated by the Greek, *ekklesia*. The *qahal* was God's people gathered together, a gathering that first took place on Sinai. The term *ekklesia* is from profane Greek and referred to the council of citizens gathered together. The Church is the gathering of the people of God called together: 'But you are a chosen race, a royal priesthood, a holy nation, God's own people' (1 Pet 2:9). The ancient origins of the Church are marvellously captured in the second vision of the Shepherd of Hermas, where the Church appears as an old woman, 'created before all things'. Other images used of the Church are: fiancée, spouse, chosen people. The Church is at once the New Jerusalem and the old woman. The Church is the fiancée, the spouse of Christ; she is the chosen people.

Church as Communion

In the past we had the image of the church as a pyramid, with the bishops on top, the priests next, then the nuns and brothers, with the laity at the bottom. The healthier image of church is to see it as a communion of all the baptised. Much more scriptural models are: Body of Christ, Sacrament of Christ, and People of God. These express our understanding of Church as communion. Those who have ordained ministries in the church (bishops, priests, deacons) are servants of that communion. The Vatican II document on priesthood, *Presbyterorum Ordinis,* situates the role and function of the ministerial priest in the context of the priesthood of the baptised (*PO* 1). This document places a strong emphasis on the ministerial priesthood as a service to the priesthood of the baptised: it is not a privilege bestowed on a few for their own benefit.

Church not Dispensable

The Year of Faith is a time of challenge to be open again to the full meaning of what it means to be Christian. Part of this is the rediscovery of the social nature of Christianity. God created humanity as a whole, not as isolated individuals. Christ came to save humanity which had become dissipated by sin. So Redemption is a social dogma. The Church is the normal locus of salvation. Whether it is through ignorance or arrogance, the 'go it alone' to God is a fraught position. We are social beings by nature; we are social by grace. We need the Church because we need Christ. As St Cyprian (d.258) wrote: 'He who does not have the Church as his mother cannot have God as his Father.'

20

How do sacraments fit in?

Noel O'Sullivan

Even people who have very little contact with Church insist on sacraments for their children: Baptism, First Confession, First Communion and Confirmation. Unfortunately, these sacraments tend more and more to be isolated events in the lives of the children and their parents, with no follow through from one sacrament to the next.

Sacraments of the Church

Sacraments are a distinctive mark of the Catholic Church. Other ecclesial communions have some sacraments – usually Baptism and Eucharist – but they are less significant than among Catholics. The whole thrust of the relationship between God and the world is sacramental. Karl Rahner (1904–84) expressed it succinctly when he proposed three levels of sacramental life. Firstly, Christ is the original or primordial sacrament of God (*Ursakrament*). Secondly, the Church, as the sacrament of Christ, is the foundational sacrament (*Grundsakrament*). Finally, we have the seven sacraments of the Church (*Sakrament*): Baptism, Confirmation, Eucharist, Penance, Sacrament of the Sick, Holy Orders and Marriage.

Rahner helped to lift the sacraments from being isolated acts and situated them within the foundational sacrament of the Church, which is founded on the primordial sacrament,

Christ. Instead of being unrelated rituals, the seven sacraments are significant moments of encounter between God and his people. In addition, they are not isolated individual encounters; they have a community dimension. Baptism is incorporation into the life of God, in the Church; Confirmation consolidates Baptism and initiates a life of witness to Christ, empowered by the Holy Spirit. Eucharist is the source and summit of the Christian life and is celebrated in community. Penance, though it seems like a private ritual, is a reconciliation with the Church and, through that reconciliation, one is reconciled to God. The sacrament of the sick is rightly celebrated in a communal setting, except in cases of necessity. Holy Orders is the sacrament whereby a man is ordained priest, bishop, or deacon. It is a sacrament given as service to the community. Marriage is easily seen as a communal event because a couple is involved but it also has a symbolic significance: it stands for the relationship between Christ and the Church (Eph 5:32).

What Does 'Sacrament' Mean?

Originally, what we call sacraments were known as mysteries, as is still the case in the Eastern Church today. The Roman lawyer, Tertullian (160–225) who introduced many Latin terms to the Church, is responsible for the term 'sacrament'. It is derived from the verb *sacrare*, meaning to swear an oath. This oath was taken, for example, when a young man entered the army. On this basis Tertullian suggested the term *sacramentum* for baptism, on entering the Church. Eventually it was applied to all the sacraments.

For St Thomas Aquinas (1225–74) the sacraments effect what they signify (*efficiunt quod figurant*). The *Catechism of the Catholic Church* defines sacraments as, 'perceptible signs (words and actions) accessible to our human nature. By the action of Christ and the power of the Holy Spirit they make present efficaciously the grace that they signify' (*CCC* 1084).

The sacramental nature of the Eucharist, for example, means that the consecrated bread and wine not only signify the death and resurrection of Christ; Christ is actually present. Participation in the Mass is the equivalent of attending the Last Supper, standing at the foot of the Cross, and being present in the garden of resurrection. In all the sacraments the grace that flows from Christ's death and resurrection is made accessible to us.

The Development of Sacraments?

We do not find the sacraments fully constituted in Scripture. What we do find is certain aspects of the ministry and preaching of Jesus which act as a basis for the sacraments. Baptism and Eucharist are easily evidenced as being instituted explicitly by Christ. However the other sacraments are more challenging in our quest for a Scriptural basis. The ministry of forgiveness and healing is a strong indicator that the Church will continue that ministry. We remember the words of Jesus to the Apostles a week after the Resurrection: 'Receive the Holy Spirit. If you forgive the sins of any, they are forgiven them; if you retain the sins of any, they are retained' (Jn 20:22ff). The sacrament of penance, as we know it today, went through many developments before it reached its present liturgical practice. In relation to the sacrament of the sick we can point to the Letter of St James (Jas 5:14–15). What is essential for us to retain is that the sacraments are rooted in Christ; they have their origin in him.

In the first millennium the number of sacraments varied between two and twelve. Those who claimed there were two sacraments were pointing to Baptism and Eucharist. For St Bernard (1890–1153) a sacrament was a sacred sign which communicated grace; washing of the feet, investiture of bishops, canons and abbots. The number of sacraments – seven – was only formally defined at the Council of Florence, in 1439.

21

Why go to Mass?

Oliver Treanor

Ireland was long known for its high attendance figures for weekly Mass. But today many find it hard to understand why they should go to Mass. What benefit has it?

To the question, 'Why should I go to Mass?' comes the simple response, 'Because Jesus asked us to do so.' 'Do this in remembrance of me', he told his disciples at the Last Supper when he instituted the Eucharist as the memorial of his death and resurrection. As he handed them the bread become his body and the chalice now become his blood, he added the poignant words, 'For you' (Lk 22:19 and 20 – i.e. repeated *twice* – and *again* in 1 Cor 11:24). Christ's presence in the Eucharist is always 'for you'. The New Testament depicts Jesus as constantly giving himself away for others – in his teaching and preaching, his healings and forgiveness, at table, on the Cross, in his coming back again to the disciples in the Resurrection – and always making his intention clear, expressing his deepest desire as '*For you, for you, for you!*'

He once described the Eucharist as the living bread. '*I am* the living bread,' he told the crowds in John's Gospel (6:51). So the gift 'for you' at Mass is himself, in person. No gift is greater than one's self. Nothing else compares, nothing is more valuable. The self that Christ shares is his crucified and risen body, the body and blood of God's Son. In the Hebrew mentality *the body* means the self just as *the blood* means one's life, and the two together comprise one's totality. So in the Eucharist the heavenly Father hands over to us the totality that Christ offered to him for us, he gives us what is most precious to him: the Beloved Child of his heart, to those who will accept him.

The Mass therefore bridges the gap of history. Without it, the Father's gift of Jesus' self-giving on Calvary would be relegated to the dusty textbooks of history. In the Eucharistic celebration Christ steps out of the past into our present, closes the gap between us, engages with our hopes and fears, and embraces us with all the divine tenderness and mercy of a Good Shepherd.

At Mass we become conscious of others who are equally loved by Christ and the Father. When God gathers each, he enfolds all. Because we now belong to him as family we also belong to each other. Together in worship we become *visibly* his Son's flesh and blood, the very same flesh and blood we receive. For in giving his body to us as the living bread Jesus makes out of us his living body the Church of which he is our head and we his bodily members – one organic, whole Christ whose identity is never complete without us. This consciousness of being-together-in-Christ breaks open the closed circles of our self-centredness. Without corporeal communion in him we develop a selfish, distorted image of ourselves, make *ourselves* gods, forget that our destiny lies in others, with and for them. We imagine ourselves alone, become lonely individuals, and lose our sense of purpose.

To receive Holy Communion, on the other hand, is to receive 'life in abundance' (Jn 10:10), the life of God himself. We become like him and we know it. But to stay away from

Mass is to distance yourself from him who is '*the* Way, *the* Truth and *the* Life' because you cannot receive the Eucharist if you are not there in the first place.

Jesus also described the Eucharist as 'the bread of life' (Jn 6:35, 48). Not just 'the *living* bread' who himself lives forever, being risen from the dead, but the *life-giving* bread who imparts the Resurrection to whoever shares his meal. 'If anyone eats of this bread,' he promised, 'he will live for ever … and I will raise him up on the last day' (Jn 6:51b; 54). This nourishment dispels our deepest fear of future extinction since it opens the mystery of transformation to us even now in the present. 'He who eats my flesh and drinks my blood,' explained Jesus, '*has* eternal life' (present continuous tense: Jn 6:54) because whoever feeds on me 'abides in me, and I abide in him' (Jn 6:56). To abide in him, having died to sin, is to be risen already, for Jesus is himself 'the Resurrection' and 'the Life' (Jn 11:25). Such intimacy of communion is quite astonishing. It means that what we suffer gives life to the world, because in the Mass it completes the sacrifice of Christ's body for the salvation of the human race (*SC*, art. 2; *LG*, art. 3). And death becomes our gateway to life, towards *permanent union* with God of which the Mass is the foretaste and promise.

Vatican II reveals the ultimate justification for going to Mass. By making present Christ's perfect worship of the Father, the liturgy is where 'God is perfectly glorified and people are sanctified' (*SC*, art. 7). Hence it rightly described the Mass as 'the source and summit of Christian existence' (*LG*, art. 11), and 'a sacred action surpassing all others (so that) no other action by us can equal its efficacy' (*SC*, art. 7).

Why go to Mass? Give me a *good* reason why not.

22

What is the significance of the 'communion of saints'?

Martin Henry

After belief in 'the holy catholic church' there is mention in the Apostles' Creed of belief in 'the communion of saints'. Are these two articles of faith simply two ways of referring to the same reality?

Is 'the holy catholic church' co-extensive with 'the communion of saints' or is there a difference between the church and the saints? It would seem that there is, if the Apostles' Creed mentions both, and not in such a way as to suggest that the second expression is merely an alternative to the previous one, or in apposition to it.

It should be said, however, that this was precisely how the Reformer, Martin Luther, understood the two expressions, namely as referring to the same reality. Even more contentious, especially since the Reformation, is the question of where the boundaries of the 'communion of saints' lie. For the Catholic tradition, the sense of the 'communion of saints' extends beyond death to those members of the church who have died and are believed to be either in heaven or in purgatory, if they need to be purified ('sanctified') before total union with God is enacted. Since the bond of communion is not broken by death, it makes sense to ask the 'saints' in heaven to intercede with God for the church on earth and in purgatory, just as it also makes sense for the church on earth to pray for the dead who are in purgatory.

As for the 'saints' themselves, they tend nowadays to be recognised as such only after their death, through a process known as 'canonization'. In their case, the old Latin saying: *de mortuis nil nisi bonum* ('speak only well of the dead') is not just a matter of good taste, but indicates the genuine sanctity and virtue the church believes the saints have attained. However that may be, in the New Testament 'the saints' referred not to the holy and virtuous deceased but to the members of various living Christian communities. Thus in many passages of the New Testament (as, for instance, 1 Cor 1:2; 2 Cor 1:1; Rom 1:7 or Acts 9:13, 32), the Christian communities on earth are described as 'the saints'. And this would tend to suggest that for the early Christians the church was indeed made up of saints, and saints alone.

Yet how does this theoretical claim square with the practical recognition that Christians don't always live what might be unequivocally called saintly lives? And the 'unsaintly' quality of many Christian lives is not an existential fact that first came to the world's attention in the later years of the church's increasingly murky history. Rather, even in the New Testament period itself, unholy quarrels among Christians themselves are unambiguously recorded, as in the case of the community in Corinth whom St Paul had to reprimand more than once (see 1 Cor 1:10–12; 2 Cor 12:20).

Moreover, the biblical witness itself, in both Testaments, rarely loses sight of human weakness and proneness to sin and err, from the Garden of Eden to the Garden of Gethsemane. The Book of Proverbs (24:16) acknowledges that even a just man can fall seven times a day, and Jesus himself reminded one of his more enthusiastic followers that, 'Only God is good' (Mk 10:18). So 'saints' can scarcely refer essentially to people with an unassailable moral character. What else might it refer to?

The writings of St Paul speak of the saints as those who have been 'sanctified in Christ Jesus and called to be his holy people' (1 Cor 1:2), or as those 'who are loved by God and called to be saints' (Rom 1:7). Hence, it would seem that the decisive clue to the meaning of Christian 'saints' is not in the first instance the quality of their moral life in itself, but rather the fact of their being 'called' by God to share in the divine life in union with Christ. Ideally, a morally admirable life would be expected to flow from such a 'calling', but it only flows from it, it is not a prerequisite for receiving it. In this sense, the original episcopal motto of Pope Francis (*miserando atque eligendo*: 'showing mercy and choosing' – a comment in a homily by the Venerable Bede for the Feast of St Matthew), catches the essence of 'sainthood' or 'sanctity'.

What is more, the 'communion' of the saints is what is paramount, since individuals don't receive their 'calling' just for their own specific benefit or perfection, but rather as a gift that is meant to be received for the good of the whole community. Indeed it can only make sense in this context, a context in which 'no man is an island'. And it can only flourish as intended if it serves the communal goal of giving glory to God, the source of all 'sanctity'.

It has often been noted that the original Latin expression for the 'communion of saints', namely *communio sanctorum*, is itself ambiguous, in that it can refer to both a communion of 'holy persons' or 'holy things'. But even if one were to interpret the phrase in the less frequent sense of 'holy things', the notion of the 'communion of holy things' still illuminates what is at stake when one tries to think together 'church' and 'sanctity'. For the 'holy things' that are 'shared' include the sacraments through which the 'saints' are called into membership of the church, the body of Christ, and strengthened in their roles therein (see 1 Cor 12).

23

What about women in the Church?

Mary McCaughey

What is the role of women in the Church? If women in the Catholic Church cannot be ordained, it seems for many that they do not have a role that is noteworthy. How then can we understand women's contribution in the Church and how is it unique?

Firstly, all human beings, both male and female are created equal in the image and likeness of the Triune God of love. The Church continues Christ's work of salvation in the world helping both men and women to grow into the likeness of Christ, *the* image of God. Through Word and sacrament all in the Church grow in building relationships of mutual giving and receptivity in love in the world.

Secondly, without wanting to stereotype female characteristics, women make a distinctive contribution in the Church and to God's plan of salvation to restore all humanity to himself. In his letter on the Dignity and Vocation of Women, *Mulieris Dignitatem* (1988), Pope John Paul II spoke of 'women's genius' in the Church. The 2004 letter, 'On the Collaboration of Men and Women in the Church and the World' explains that while all in the Church are called to reflect Christ, women have a 'capacity for the other' that is somehow linked to their physical capacity to give life, to be mothers.

The Church is not here determining women's identity in terms of their biology. Rather, it means that the intellectual, psychological and social dispositions which accompany a physical capacity for motherhood represent a uniquely feminine way of relating to others. This applies even to those Christian women who are single for the kingdom and those consecrated to virginity. God becomes their primary 'other', thus fulfilling their desire for self-gift in love and leading to a different type of motherhood, 'of the Spirit' (*MD*, 21) expressed in motherly love for other people, especially the most vulnerable. This is not to say that women, like men do not also manifest many other gifts such as the gift of theological scholarship, administration, leadership and teaching, yet all these gifts are also informed by a feminine approach for the good of the Church and the world.

Women in a particular way represent the Church as Bride and Mother. This point also helps explain why women are not ordained in the Catholic Church. Catholic theology explains that at the Mass, the ministerial priest represents Christ the Bridegroom offering his body and blood for his Bride the Church. While every human being in the Church whether male or female is called to represent the Church as Bride and respond to Christ's love with the gift of self (*MD*, 25), in Scriptures, the Bride of the covenant is represented by women. Mary as the Mother of God, embodies this nuptial relationship, representing the Church as Bride in a completely unsurpassable way as divinity and humanity are united in her womb.

To be Bride and Mother in the image of Mary, does not reduce a woman's place in the Church to passivity in relation to men, but is rather about relating to God in a nuptial way by grace, which then moves to action. This is not to say that through history women have not suffered from a lack of appreciation of their efforts to contribute to Church life.

Thus, often and understandably, women's attempt to claim their place in the Church is focused on achieving a right to ministerial priesthood rather than one that emphasizes her unique living of the common priesthood as the offering of her life and gifts.

Conceived without sin, Mary is full of grace and completely without any obstacle in her communion with the Triune God. In her virgin-motherhood, she reveals the nature of the common priesthood for both men and women based on a self-offering which gives glory to God. This self-offering is rooted in a continual conversion towards Christ, fostering an ever-deeper union with him. It gives glory to God by fruitful love, as mother and as life-giver.

The 'feminine genius' reflects the Marian dimension of the Church in a unique way, without which the Church could not adequately conceptualise and live its vocation to love in the world. The feminine charism is based on fostering and nurturing union with Christ so that Christ is truly brought to birth in the life of all members of the Church. It offers insights for faith in the family, parishes, ecclesial movements, dioceses and is to shape the highest levels of theology, Church decision making and formulation of doctrine. When the feminine charism is recognised, hierarchical structures of communion in the Church can more adequately support divine life and grace at the heart of the Church in a way that is most attentive to what is fully human and life-giving. For this and for the ongoing renewal of ecclesial life, the uniqueness of women's contribution is to adequately inform life in the Church from its core outwards.

24

What happens after our death?

Mary McCaughey

The death of a loved one begs us to ask whether we can ever hope to see them again. Does the meaning of life and love simply end in the grave? What does our Christian faith say to us about what happens after death?

A famous philosopher, Ludwig Feuerbach, once accused Christians of focusing too much on getting to heaven, and neglecting their call in this life to build up the Kingdom of God. Another philosopher, Martin Heidegger said that to live an authentic life, human beings needed to constantly reflect on death. Yet neither philosopher could offer any hope to us that there could be life beyond death. Early Christians in the Catacombs portrayed Christ with a Gospel and a philosopher's staff. Christ was *the* philosopher as he offered an answer to the question of what happened after death.

On the Cross, suffering towards his death, Jesus promised the good thief, 'This day you will be with me in Paradise' (Lk 23:43). For Christians, our hope of eternal life with Christ beyond death is based on a certain promise which is connected to the event of our Baptism, since 'if we have died with Christ, then we shall also live with him' (Rom 6:8). Death from a Christian perspective is not merely a biological event, but a metaphysical one, speaking to us of our destiny, and the mystery of eternity. Since Christ has entered into human death and triumphed over its power, then Christians enter into the mystery of death in a completely new way.

What happens after our death is indeed a mystery. 'Heaven is the state of supreme, definitive happiness' (CCC 1024) where God is beheld, 'face to face'. Yet heaven is not just a future state of which we can know nothing. Rather it can be understood as the final consummation of the Christian life of loving union with God and others. It is a unity that we can taste even now through sharing the Eucharist and living charity in the Holy Spirit. The Carmelite blessed, Elizabeth of the Trinity, recognised this reality in a more interior way in her own experience when she wrote, 'I have found heaven, for heaven is God and God is in my soul.'

If God is truly compassionate and merciful to sinners, why bother discussing hell or purgatory? While God in his infinite love, could not desire that any human being be separated from him for all eternity, in theory a state of complete separation from God and others could be freely chosen by us. Purgatory testifies to God's merciful love which desires to bring us to communion with himself. In the light of his loving gaze we experience the pain of remorse and shame for our unloving behaviour, until eventually we can meet that gaze with untroubled joy.

To accept the doctrine of Hell is to accept the possibility of a place of eternal isolation from God and others after death. The early Church Fathers, Origen and Gregory of Nyssa, believed in *apocatastasis*: that all things and human beings will be saved at the end and God could not abandon anyone to hell after death. Since Christ himself has entered into every human abandonment caused by freely-chosen sin, even descending into hell, it surely illustrates that

God's love reaches to the furthest depths of this separation from God? Surely we cannot say that hell still exists? While the Church teaches that hell exists as God's positive judgment over evil, it can never say that anyone is actually in hell. As the Youth Catechism, *YouCat* puts it, 'we do not know whether anyone at the moment of death can look absolute love in the face and still say no!' Yet the Gospel warns us to make proper use of our freedom and not to separate ourselves definitively from God by shutting our hearts against the needs of our neighbour (Mt 25:41–45).

Christians believe in the Resurrection of the Body at the last day because of our understanding that human beings express their very humanity through their bodies. Hence human redemption cannot simply be of our souls alone. Nor do Christians believe in Reincarnation. My personal soul cannot be reincarnated in another material body but is made for my personal body alone: this unity makes me 'me'. Mary as the first of the new creation, foreshadows this mystery in her Assumption, where she is taken in the unity of her body and soul into heaven.

Christians believe that at the end of time, at an hour that only the Father knows, Christ will return in glory. At this hour, the truth of our thoughts, deeds and relationships with others will be brought into God's light. God's plan of salvation will be unveiled, showing how through his acts of Providence in history, he has led creation towards its final end. Until the new heavens and the new earth are established, the Church exists as a sign or 'sacrament' of this final unity offering peace, joy and fulfilment to the human heart which awaits that consummation in the life beyond death.

25

Do we still believe in Purgatory?

Oliver Treanor

Years ago there was a strong emphasis on purgatory. There seems to be less talk about it in recent times. Do we still believe in purgatory nowadays, and if so why?

Yes we certainly do, and with good reason. The fact that we set aside November 2nd as a day of solemn commemoration and intercession for the dead, starting a month of intense prayer for them every year, shows how concerned Catholics are for their departed brothers and sisters. You don't pray for the saints in glory, nor for the demons in hell; therefore prayer for the faithful departed implies an in-between state after death – not yet heaven, certainly not hell – where the deceased we love may still be waiting for the fulness of salvation not yet attained.

Though Sacred Scripture is not explicit about purgatory, it is not silent either. Reading between the lines of Holy Writ, purgatory is a very logical deduction to make. Even the *Old* Testament affirmed that 'it is a holy and wholesome thought to pray for the dead that they may be loosed from their sins' (2 Mac 12:46) – a text quoted by Vatican II in its teaching on the last things (*LG*, art. 50). The *New* Testament ends with the great vision of heaven where 'nothing unclean shall enter the holy city'; and yet the Letter to the

Hebrews reports a vast multitude there of 'just men who have *been made perfect'* (12:22–23). Given that most of us are far from perfect yet not so bad as to deserve damnation, where does this *cleansing* take place, this *being made perfect*? Certainly not always in this present life. While the Bible does not supply a direct answer the Church does, and *has* done consistently both in her doctrinal teaching and liturgical custom. Since revelation reaches us through Sacred Tradition as well as through Scripture, we have sure ground for believing what the Church has always taught from the beginning: firstly that purgatory exists; secondly that we can ease the pain there by offering Christ's sacrifice in the Mass for the deceased, by almsgiving on their behalf and other works of piety like visits to the cemetery or the parish church in November.

Although the pain of purgatory derives from the longing for God, for a share in his glory through the blissful vision of his face, yet it is completely distinct from the torment of hell. Whereas damnation is eternal separation, irreparable loss, purgatory prepares the soul for ultimate union with the Trinity in perfect joy. Therefore these souls are said to be at peace with their suffering. They accept it willingly for God's sake and so even now are called 'holy' – the Holy Souls.

Just what form this purgation might take and its precise purpose is a matter of conjecture, given that this aspect of the faith is veiled, being 'of eternity' rather than 'of time'. In the west for example, the Latin Church has tended to see purgatory as a retribution, a satisfaction for sin through purification and cleansing. The Orthodox east, by contrast, think of it as a spiritual growth towards maturity. Both possibilities resonate with our ways of thinking today. On the one hand we understand legal judgments and penalties; on the other, we also understand personal counselling and human growth therapy. All of these involve pain, but all are ordered towards a positive outcome.

Whichever way we think of purgatory, one thing is clear. Healing, purification, growth, maturation is achieved by the flame of Christ's love for the sinner. Death configures the soul definitively to Christ's Cross. It completes the sign of baptism by which we die with him, are buried with him and share his risen life. How then could Christ meet such a soul and not be moved? Indeed, when we die where else is there for us to go other than to that Love from whom we come? Might we not say then that just as God's presence is heaven for those who love in return, but hell for those who despise him, so it is sweet pain for those not yet perfected in charity, and who know it?

Fifty years ago the Second Vatican Council enlarged our thinking about life after death by focusing attention not so much on the fate of the individual soul but on the broad scope of God's great plan of salvation for all his elect. It described the Church as a pilgrim people, en route together to Christ who is the Alpha and the Omega. He is the Church's destiny, the terminating point of all creation, of history and of each individual soul. Grace is dispensed through the Church as the universal sacrament of salvation because it is the body of Christ himself. Therefore whoever remains in the bosom of the Church, in communion with all her members, sharing the same Spirit, believing in the same Lord, following the same Gospel, has nothing to fear from death or from purgatory. We remain in the Church whether we live or die so that then, as now, we will always be the children of salvation, inheritors of the prize of the communion of saints.

26

What is the Church saying about Ecology?

Mary McCaughey

While we know that Christianity obliges us to care for our fellow human beings, does the Church say anything to us about caring for creation and the natural environment? If it does, are we then obliged to take the ecological crisis seriously? Does it mean cultivating a simpler lifestyle; conserving water, refraining from using aerosols or fossil fuels; walking and cycling instead of driving; using recycled paper and no plastic packaging? Why bring God into it?

The Church calls Christians to respect for the natural environment since God is the Creator of the universe including all species of life from plants and animals to human beings. The world is endowed with order and harmony reflecting his glory (Rom 1:20) and we know from the Genesis creation stories that all that God created was 'good' (Gen 1:31). God also gave man and woman the responsibility to care for creation. However, the command to 'have dominion over the fish of the sea, the birds of the air, and all the living things that move on the earth' (Gen 1:28) has often been misinterpreted to justify the reckless use of resources rather than encouraging men and women to be tenders of creation. This has contributed in no small way to an ecological crisis. St Francis of Assisi, the Church's patron of the environment, reminds us of the vision of faith needed to see the environment as God's gift to us. We are to care for it accordingly and refrain from abusing its resources.

There has been a gradual re-awakening in the view that the progress of humanity can only be one which is in harmony with nature and the natural world. As Pope Benedict XVI emphasized in his encyclical, *Caritatis in Veritate*, 'The way humanity treats the environment influences the way it treats itself, and vice versa' (*CV*, 51). Working to overcome ecological problems has a positive impact on the economic and cultural underdevelopment of peoples.

Today however there can be a tendency to over-correct the respect due to the environment in a way that neglects a legitimate attention to human beings and their rational ability to relate responsibly to that creation (*CV*, 48). Yet, the Church has always taught that the human being holds the centre position within the ecosystem. Psalm 8 proclaims the dignity of the human being: 'you have made him little less than a god, with glory and honour you crowned him.' Human reason and skill is used to reach agreement about the use of scarce natural resources such as water and overcoming problems such as desertification in the natural environment. Thus when 'human ecology is respected within society, environmental ecology also benefits' (*CV*, 51).

The ecological crisis is closely linked to the notion of development itself. It therefore is connected to our understanding of human beings and their relationship to others and to the rest of creation. To protect the overall ecological balance of creation, the decisive issue for the Church is the overall moral tenor of society affecting how we see the place of human beings in this balance. Firstly, as Pope Benedict noted in his 2012 message for World Day of Peace, there is a need for a lifestyle 'which is marked by a certain sobriety and solidarity'. Secondly, it is contradictory to insist that future generations respect the natural environment when our educational systems and laws do not help them to respect themselves and their dignity as human beings as part of this ecosystem. As *Caritas in Veritate* makes clear, if there is a lack of respect for the right to life and to a natural death, if human conception, gestation and birth are made artificial, if human embryos are sacrificed to research, the conscience of society ends up losing the concept of human ecology and, along with it, that of environmental ecology (*CV*, 51). Ecology takes in not only the environment but also human life, sexuality, marriage, the family, social relations. All of these issues relate to integral human development.

While our Christian call to care for the ecological balance of nature is linked to our duties towards the human person, considered in oneself and in relation to others, it is also about our duty to God. It calls us to uphold the order that God has inscribed in the world. Since God is the source of truth and love (*CV*, 52), for Christians there can only be authentic balance in the created order if God's design in creation is upheld. As Pope John Paul II stated in his message for the 1990 World Day of Peace when 'man turns his back on the Creator's plan, he provokes a disorder which has inevitable repercussions on the rest of the created order.' Pope John Paul II concludes his message with mention of St Francis of Assisi who, he says, 'gives us striking witness that when we are at peace with God, we are better able to devote ourselves to building up that peace with all creation which is inseparable for peace among all God's people'. Pope Francis has drawn inspiration from St Francis' example. In his first homily he spoke of the vocation to be 'protectors'. This 'means protecting all creation, the beauty of the created world, as the Book of Genesis tells us and as Saint Francis of Assisi showed us. It means respecting each of God's creatures and respecting the environment in which we live'.

27

Does the Church still believe in the 'Second Coming' of Christ?

Martin Henry

The Apostles' Creed speaks about Christ coming at an unspecified time 'to judge the living and the dead'. This is usually taken to refer to the 'second coming' of Christ. But what does the 'second coming' really mean, and what is the current status of this belief?

According to an ancient Christian adage (*lex orandi, lex credendi*, a phrase that could be roughly translated as: 'the law of prayer is the law of belief'), the church's traditional worship or liturgy can be regarded as a reliable guide to its belief. Thus, when two of the three possible acclamations after the consecration, in the new translation of the Mass, include a reference to the 'second coming' ('... until you come again'), as does the third Eucharistic prayer ('and as we look forward to his second coming'), and the prayer after the Our Father ('as we await the blessed hope and the coming of our saviour, Jesus Christ'), the self-evident conclusion would seem to be that belief in Christ's 'second coming' is unquestionably part of the church's faith.

But in the case of the doctrine of the 'second coming', has the *lex credendi* somehow become disconnected from the *lex orandi*? It might be useful to begin trying to answer this question by asking what exactly the 'second coming' referred to when it was undoubtedly a vital aspect of Christian belief, in contrast to the contemporary church's seemingly rather muted sense of the doctrine.

A pertinent illustration of pristine Christian faith in the imminence of the 'second coming' can be found in St Paul's First Letter to the Thessalonians (4:15–17). The gospels too point to this early belief (Mt 24:42–44; Lk 12:39–40), and, as is well known, it is most naturally at home in the last book of the New Testament, The Apocalypse (Revelation), specifically at Rev 19:11–16. This was the book of the Bible that Marx's friend Engels declared to be 'worth more than the rest of the New Testament put together', presumably because it was about hope for the future, a commodity that Marxism was also very interested in.

Apart from the 'second coming', other expressions, like 'the Day of the Lord' or the Greek term *parousia* (meaning in Greek both 'presence' and 'coming'), were used in the New Testament to refer to the final reality that the early Christians looked forward eagerly to participating in, when the entire cosmos would be transfigured and God would be 'all in all' (1 Cor 15:28).

Yet if the early Christians were awaiting an imminent end of all history, their hopes were not in fact fulfilled in any literal sense. And some of the early Christians themselves appear to have been already well aware of this potentially embarrassing problem. Thus, in 2 Peter 3:8 one hears a clear echo of an early attempt to 'explain away', so to speak, the problem of the *parousia* which hasn't yet happened: '[W]ith the Lord one day is as a thousand years.' With such an explanation, the acuteness of the problem could be somewhat attenuated, but the problem still remained.

One aspect of the 'second coming' that was to attain great significance in the history of Christianity, especially in the Middle Ages, was the question of 'chiliasm' (from the Greek word for a 'thousand') or 'millenarianism' (from the Latin word for a 'thousand'). This was a belief, based on Rev 20:1–15, that Christ would return before the Last Judgement, and rule with the risen saints for a thousand years before the final End would come. This intriguing chapter of The Book of Revelation exercised the theological ingenuity of many of the Fathers of the Church, some interpreting it more literally, others in a more spiritual direction. St Augustine 'identified the thousand-year reign with the period between Christ's resurrection and his return' (Wolfgang Beinert and Francis Schüssler Fiorenza, eds, *Handbook of Catholic Theology*, p. 70), in other words with the time of the church, and interpreted the idea of 'a thousand years' not literally but, rather, symbolically.

Catholic thinkers, however, became increasingly wary of the notion of millenarianism, since it had provided support for some of the wilder expressions of discontent with current social, economic, political and religious circumstances in later ages (see Norman Cohn, *The Pursuit of the Millennium*). Thus the 'Catholic theologians of the Counter-Reformation period rejected as erroneous even a mitigated chiliasm, that is, the acceptance of an interim period in which the risen martyrs and confessors will reign with Christ on earth' (*Handbook of Catholic Theology*, p. 70). Finally, in 1944, a 'decree of the Holy Office … stated that even a mitigated chiliasm cannot be taught as certain' (*ibid.*).

The Holy Office, as it was then known, might have been swayed in its decision by the startling reappearance of 'chiliasm' in the West in the shape of the Nazi ideology of the Third Reich, referred to by its supporters as the 'Thousand-Year Reich'. The grip of apocalyptic imagery on the Western imagination is reflected also in the title and dramatic language of one of W.B. Yeats's most famous poems, 'The Second Coming'.

While misunderstandings of the 'second coming' will probably always recur, this should not be allowed to undermine the fundamentally unchanging truth of the credal formulation itself. This is simply the belief that the world is both created and redeemed through the Word of God. In the world's beginning lies also its end. Christ's 'second coming' (not to be understood numerically or temporally, as the early Christians seem to have imagined) is the affirmation of God's final triumphant victory over sin and death in Christ that enacts the eternal salvation of his creation.